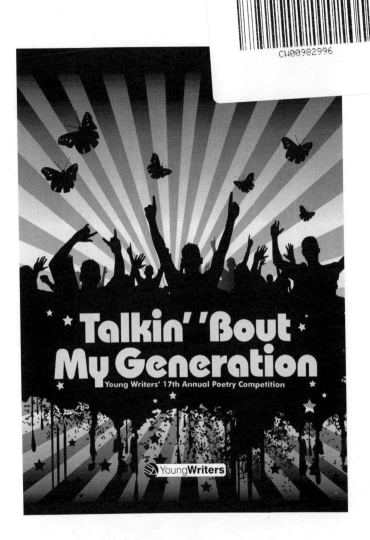

Talkin' 'Bout My Generation
Young Writers' 17th Annual Poetry Competition

YoungWriters

Bedfordshire & Cambridgeshire
Edited by Donna Samworth

CW00982996

 Young**Writers**

First published in Great Britain in 2008 by:
Young Writers
Remus House
Coltsfoot Drive
Peterborough
PE2 9JX
Telephone: 01733 890066
Website: www.youngwriters.co.uk

All Rights Reserved

© Copyright Contributors 2008

SB ISBN 978-1 84431 506 2

Foreword

This year, the Young Writers' *Talkin' 'Bout My Generation* competition proudly presents a showcase of the best poetic talent selected from thousands of up-and-coming writers nationwide.

Young Writers was established in 1991 to promote the reading and writing of poetry within schools and to the young of today. Our books nurture and inspire confidence in the ability of young writers and provide a snapshot of poems written in schools and at home by budding poets of the future.

The thought, effort, imagination and hard work put into each poem impressed us all and the task of selecting poems was a difficult but nevertheless enjoyable experience.

We hope you are as pleased as we are with the final selection and that you and your family continue to be entertained with *Talkin' 'Bout My Generation Bedfordshire & Cambridgeshire* for many years to come.

Contents

Brooklands Middle School, Leighton Buzzard

Challney High School for Boys, Luton

Hastingsbury School, Kempston

Simone Demetriou (12)	70
Emily Lunny (12)	71
Charlotte Field (12)	72
Alexander King (12)	73
Bethany Darville (12)	74
Megan Pope (12)	75
Hannah Taylor (12)	76
Sam Hall (12)	77
Jordan Milnthorpe (12)	78
Katie Clements (12)	79
Harry Yardy (12)	80
Laurence Twell (12)	81

Northfields Technology College, Dunstable

Anthony East (15)	81
Shianele Abraham (13)	82
Rhys Stevens (13)	82
Ryan Jefcoate (14)	83
Kelly Ayliffe (14)	83
Charlotte Cootes (13)	84
Stephen Cobb (15)	84
Devon Kears (13)	85
Jordan Back (13)	85
Tom Wade (14)	86
Ben White (14)	87
Ben Harper (13)	88
Michael Johnston (15)	88
Jacob Kyte (13)	89
Kayleigh Goodridge (14)	89
Megan McMahon (13)	90
Ellie Doherty (13)	90
Luke Holdstock (13)	91
Taylor Wallace (13)	91
Jayne Aris (14)	92
Ashley Bloomfield (15)	92
Nadine Sharp (15)	92
Kabelan Karunaseelan (13)	93
Kristen James (15)	93
Andrew East (15)	93
Penny Mitchell (14)	94
Danniel Owen (13)	94

Chris Dawkins (13)	95
Christopher Downes (13)	95
Adam Ilsley (13)	96
Tom Allmett (13)	97
Guy Rayment (13)	97

Peterborough High School, Peterborough

Eloise Austin (12)	98
Sidney Thomas (12)	99
Megan Chittock (13)	100
Megan Orme-Smith (13)	101
Grace Sandys (13)	102
Lucy Blatchford (12)	103
Florentyne Barrett (13)	104
Anoushka Edirisooriya (13)	104
Pooja Seta (12)	105
Holly Lawler (11)	105
Bethany Cameron (12)	106
Gemma Rate (13)	107
Katie Ivens (11)	108
Chloe King (13)	108
Molly Adam (13)	109
Micheala Drazek (12)	109
Ji Young Hwang (13)	110
Hannah Diver (13)	111
Lucille Kenny (12)	112
Ellie Raby-Smith (12)	113
Victoria Thorpe Jones (12)	114
Zara Tosh (13)	115
Bethany Johnson (13)	116
Sophie Wilson (12)	117
Emily Yong (14)	118
Aarti Patel (13)	119
Susannah Lewis (14)	120
Ellie Wood (13)	121
Tabitha McNulty-Skead (11)	122
Becky Dennis (14)	123
Chloë Laycock (11)	124
Simran Kaur Nanuwa (11)	125
Pavna Venugopal (11)	126
Katie Jeffs (13)	127

Bethan Youens (12)	128
Sheringham Reynolds (12)	129
Sehar Nazir (11)	130
Marya Yousaf (11)	131
Hollie Ismail (12)	132
Ruth Plant (13)	133
Emma Heys (11)	134
Ellie-Rose Fowler (11)	135
Sreejoyee Roychowdhury (11)	136
Imogen Hallett (12)	136
Serena Ward (12)	137
Natasha van Uden (13)	137
Katie Parkin (12)	138
Becci Jeffers (12)	139
Charlotte Shoemake (12)	139

Sawston Village College, Sawston

Hannes Whittingham (13)	140
Duncan MacGregor (11)	141
Jake Hardwick (12)	142
George Chapman (12)	142
Amy Ornstien (13)	143
Cassie Cope (12)	143
Alex Batten (13)	144
Emily Morris (11)	144
Philipp Scholtes (11)	145
Connor Ellis (12)	145
Katie Lloyd (11)	146
Jordan Smart (11)	146
Anna Tindall (12)	147
Ellis Stratton (11)	147
Jack Hayden (12)	148
Megan Salmon (12)	148
Evelyn Roddom (11)	149
Fiona Case (12)	149
Vivien Gu (11)	150
Emma Mounsey (11)	150
Tom Lucas (12)	151
Eleanor Fish (11)	151
Áine Jones (12)	152
William Ingram (12)	152

Adam Sear (14)   178
Sophie Harris (15)   179
Zuhair Crossley (13)   180
Eleanor Eloya (11)   180
Carl Sadler (13)   181

Woodland Middle School, Flitwick
Emma Bright (11)   181
Phoebe Wilsmore (11)   182
Frankie Finn (12)   183
Luke Browne (12)   184
Thomas Harrison (11)   184
Holly Barber (11)   185
Ellena Gazeley (11)   185
Victoria Abbott (11)   186
Nick Welton (11)   187
Katie Veryard (11)   188
Charlotte Haimes (12)   189

The Poems

The Hairy Monster

Have you ever wondered if we were all alone?
Because some kind of lifeform is living in my wardrobe.

When I turn out my light I think it's going to pounce,
But truthfully it settles down and soon I hear him snore.

Early in the morning I went to get a drink,
To find a hairy monster rummaging through my fridge.

I gave a little screech but it really didn't work,
As the very hairy monster gave a very loud burp.

When he'd eaten all the contents of our gigantic fridge,
The very hairy monster just went back to bed!

Charlotte Blythe (11)
Brooklands Middle School, Leighton Buzzard

My War Poem

Rotting skin, dying breath
Smothered all over the battlefield
Soldiers suffering and turning to the sky
Families crying as their dad passes by
One gun fires, another life ends
The sound of a rifle brings pain to the men.

If you were there you'd never hear yourself plot
You'd have to make a move or you'd go down to rot
Life is a whistle that can go in a flash
So take good care or it will go with a crash.

Kieran Taylor (12)
Brooklands Middle School, Leighton Buzzard

Gun Shootings And Car Accidents

The day I left the hospital at Lewsey Farm
was the biggest mistake of my life.
Gunshots and car accidents are a part of my life
and this is my story.
A friend could be here one day and gone the next.
The thing that holds our friendship together
was shattered by a piece of metal fired out of a gun.
The very thing that made you friends can make you enemies.
There is so much left to do in your lifetime
and could devastate your life forever.
A car accident could be great or horrible,
it all depends on whose side you're on.
Can you handle being shot or would you run?
If you don't have a choice to run?
A true friend has no meaning in Lewsey Farm.
You could have 2 friends or none but everyone has enemies.
You could be playing in the park with your friends
or on your way to the shop.
You fly over the bonnet of a car.
Is it your fault your friends hurt or is it theirs?
But that is the thing that made me snap.
People said that I was a coward for leaving my home.
I waved goodbye to my friends and frowned at my enemies
and thought, *it's finally over.*

Richard Batten (13)
Brooklands Middle School, Leighton Buzzard

Life Of A Boxer

The boxer sweats, he feels the heat
He has to train, he does not eat
But bear in mind he skips all day
He wants to make it all the way
To make the final would be a dream
To make the final would make his smile gleam.

Callum Dobie (12)
Brooklands Middle School, Leighton Buzzard

Iraq War

Slowly walking through the mud
All I see is lots of red blood

Lying there in my trench
There's a revolting stench

Thinking about how I'm a bomber
When I die I'll be in honour

Seeing other young soldiers in Iraq
How they are brave
Sorry to say they'll be in their grave

Winning, we are determined
But not when there's lots of vermin

While the world is eroding . . .
All I hear is bombs exploding

My family sitting on a steep hill crying
Surrounded by thoughts . . .
That I might be dying!

A phone call made to my family
To tell them that I am . . . *dead!*

Jodie Molloy (12)
Brooklands Middle School, Leighton Buzzard

My School

There is a school that they are trying to shut down.
There are kids that love that school like it was their own.
There is a bunch of people fighting, singing and shouting
for that school not to be closed,
that is the reason I am writing this poem.
So please don't shut down Brooklands Middle School.
I am a fighter because I thought this was the school for me.

Denzil Guwa (12)
Brooklands Middle School, Leighton Buzzard

War

My guilty heart is heavily beating
Unlike the bodies that I'm meeting.

The painful cries of all my friends
The heartbreaking message that it sends.

Why are we fighting?
We should be reuniting.

The blasts don't stop and neither do the guns
Now the gas starts entering my lungs!

Now it really is the end
So goodbye and good luck my dear old friend.

Michael Gibbins (12)
Brooklands Middle School, Leighton Buzzard

Football

Walking through the terrifying tunnel
Like a nervous wreck,
It's my first game for Shiverpool
I don't know what to do.
The game has just began.
The ball has come to me.
It's all a blur
I cannot see.
Bang!
What can this be?
Oh my god, my leg's in three!

Peter Wilmer (12)
Brooklands Middle School, Leighton Buzzard

Phantom

It walks around the room careless
Scaring people as it stares
There's something different
It changes every day
Different face, different clothes
I see it every night
First time I was scared
But now it's come a few times
It's alright to walk around
All it does is stare
Nothing really different
Except its face and clothes
The second time I saw it I thought it was a different person
Until I got to know him
He was the same person all the time.

Daniel Holloway (10)
Brooklands Middle School, Leighton Buzzard

Generation

G reat as it sounds
E very generation has a downside
N ot always the same downside though
E ven today we are fighting against this downside
R eally important that we stop it.
A nd it depends on our daily life
T his is true
I t's called global warming
O therwise, if we don't stop it
N othing will exist on this planet.

Sam Roberts (13)
Brooklands Middle School, Leighton Buzzard

Angel Of Death

My friends say I'm schizophrenic,
But at the moment, I'm euphoric.

I'm lying dirty, dishevelled amongst the bins,
Smoking and sniffing, my throbbing head begins to spin.

An hour ago, the grubby needle pierced my arm,
Does this really do much harm?

Eyes watering, mouth drooling,
My blood is spurting.

My heart skips a beat,
As I trip over my feet.

The lights are fading and so am I,
Slowly my heart is stopping, I am about to die.

Rebecca Ranson (12)
Brooklands Middle School, Leighton Buzzard

Animal Cruelty

A nimals
N eed
I nexplicable
M aintaining
A nd
L ove

C herish
R espect
U nderstand and
E mbrace
L ife's
T iny
Y ouths.

Laura Buckingham (12)
Brooklands Middle School, Leighton Buzzard

The War Of The Dead

War is a violent hurricane of firing bullets.
The battlefield is a giant global graveyard, full of honourable souls.
No-man's-land is a flood of blood and gore.
Life at war is a life of misery and . . . certain death.
Fighting to the death is a ghastly nightmare coming to life.
There is a constant hail of gunfire and explosions.
It is a place of death, disease and suicide.
War is a time in which you find . . . *no mercy!*

Conor Goodger (12)
Brooklands Middle School, Leighton Buzzard

Cat

Fence climber
Fish finder

Bird catcher
Fly snatcher

Rat stalkers
Street walkers

Scary hisser
Lovely kisser

Ball bouncer
Mouse pouncer

Night sleeper
Fish food eater

Dog hater
Kitten crater

One lovely cat.

Kieran Goodger (10)
Brooklands Middle School, Leighton Buzzard

Save The Poor

S uggest something fantastic
A suggestion to help
V ista the life and day of them
E veryone points and smirks at them, but I don't.

T hey have had something taken away
H ere we are in our warm beds
E ach day they have cold hard ground as their beds.

P oorness is bad, terrible, disgusting
O h why did God make me poor?
O h why are there poor in the world?
R emember those who need it more,
    and who deserve it more.

Stuart Till (11)
Brooklands Middle School, Leighton Buzzard

Cats

Cats catch mice,
They think they're nice.
Running about the house all day,
They take a catnap in the hay.
Cats lay on your bed at night,
Because they like the light.
They lounge about in the sun,
They think it's great fun.
They have loads of chums,
Because they like to hum.
Cats chase leaves,
They decide to weave.
In and out of weeds,
On a bright red lead.

Alice Till (10)
Brooklands Middle School, Leighton Buzzard

I Am A Soldier

I am a soldier
I live in a trench
I just woke up
To see my friend dead

I get on with the day
To fight for my trade
Until the day fades

I am a soldier
I live in a trench
I just woke up
To see my friend dead

It came to nightfall
I looked out the trench to find everyone dead
I'm all alone
And not sure of the way home

I am a soldier
I live in a trench
I just woke up
To see everyone dead.

Symone Hodge (12)
Brooklands Middle School, Leighton Buzzard

I Am A Dog

I am a dog, alone and scared
Watching people, they stir and stir
I live in a field, I sleep in the grass
I don't know when I ate last.
I want a family, I want a home
I want somewhere to call my home
I want somewhere I can stay
I want somewhere I can play.

Michael Dunne (11)
Brooklands Middle School, Leighton Buzzard

I'm A Soldier

I'm a soldier,
With a folder,
Full of rats,
The size of cats.

I can see a bumblebee,
Slimy slug,
With a bug.

I'm getting old
And freezing cold,
But tension not,
Same old strength,
Live in a trench.

I'm feeling unhappy,
Missing my family,
Feeling so glum,
Just had some rum.

I'm a soldier,
With a folder,
Full of rats,
The size of cats.

I smell so bad,
That people go mad,
I smell of pee
And my name is Ashley.

I have to lie,
But cannot cry,
As my parents are ill,
And they're having pills.

Zarish Aslam (12)
Brooklands Middle School, Leighton Buzzard

I Am A Soldier

I am a soldier
I live in a trench
I hide under a park bench
I am nearly always in a mess

I used to be weak and unhealthy at home

I am a soldier
I live in a trench
I hide under a park bench
I am nearly always in a mess

I miss my mum and my family
I miss going to school and coming back

I am a soldier
I live in a trench
I hide under a park bench
I am nearly always in a mess

I scream, I talk
I curse and swear

So don't come near to me
Or I'll shout and scream

All I want is to be free

Can't you understand!

Rebecca Seston (12)
Brooklands Middle School, Leighton Buzzard

I Am A Soldier

I'm a soldier.
I live on a campsite.
I'm nearly always in my tent.

I used to go out and fight
But now can't.
But I did try and fight again,
Then I got hit.

I tried to get away but they got me,
Then I went to my tent and found my mate dead.

I haven't eaten for a few days.
I'm hungry and I need to eat but I need to fight as well.

I went to bed
But then I heard a noise,
I jumped up and ran out of my tent,
I found someone dead.

Zoe Flatt (12)
Brooklands Middle School, Leighton Buzzard

If I Was An Heiress

If I was an heiress
I wouldn't be big-headed,
I would save my money up for something worth it.
I wouldn't make a fuss
Unless I really must.
I wouldn't starve myself so I won't turn to dust.

If I was an heiress
I would be pretty and witty
I would buy myself a kitty called City,
We would live together forever.

Shannon Butler (12)
Brooklands Middle School, Leighton Buzzard

The Soldier

I'm a soldier
I live in a zoo
I'm nearly always
Catching the flu.

I used to be a fighter
At school I should have been brighter
Now I have to be tough and mightier

I am a soldier
I use a gun
I don't even think it's fun
I rarely see the sun.

I am a soldier
I am a soldier.

Aaron Clarke (12)
Brooklands Middle School, Leighton Buzzard

A Soldier At War

A soldier at war
A soldier in shock
A soldier with his rifle
Shooting his flock

A soldier at war
A soldier in shock
A soldier unhappy
Missing his family
Writing a letter
Feeling better
A soldier at war
A soldier in shock.

Georgina Kaye (13)
Brooklands Middle School, Leighton Buzzard

A Soldier

I'm a soldier
I live in a trench
I'm nearly always
In a war.

I used to sit home
And speak with my family
With a nice fat roast.

I'm a soldier
I live in a trench
I'm nearly always
In a war.

I'm using a gun
To survive with rum
To take revenge
For my mum
The person that shot me
Is the person that kills me.

I'm a soldier
I live in trench
I'm nearly always
In a war.

I'm now nearing my death
Kissing my deathbed
I'm cuckoo in the head
Singing in my bed.

I am a soldier
Now I am dead!

Robert Wright (12)
Brooklands Middle School, Leighton Buzzard

I Am A Soldier

I'm a soldier
I live in a trench
I'm nearly always
On the bench

I used to be free
Now I'm nearly always
Up a tree

I'm a soldier
I live in a trench
I'm nearly always
On the bench

I miss my family
I miss my bed
And my old-fashioned shed

I'm a soldier
I live in a trench
I'm nearly always
On the bench.

I shoot, I dive
I run, I duck
I hide
So don't come near me
Or I'll shoot you in your head
Because I miss my bed.

I want to be free

Can't you understand!

Daniel Bridges (11)
Brooklands Middle School, Leighton Buzzard

What Am I?

I live in a house,
I don't eat but I drink and blink,
I'm very colourful and people use me nearly every day,
I hate the sun but I love the rain,
and
I
love
to
get
a
bath
on
a
stormy
night,
I
protect
people.
What else can I say?

What am I?

A: umbrella.

Angelika Szymanska (12)
Brooklands Middle School, Leighton Buzzard

The Abandoned Kitten

My family dumped me
They left me alone
I'm just a sweet kitten
Please give me home.

They bought me for Christmas
Got bored with me easily
So they put me in a box
Then dumped me in an alley.

I miss my mother
And my brothers too
I have no one to play with
And I can't find the loo.

I have no food to eat
It's wet, cold and dark
I sometimes hear noises
Like an old dog's bark.

I live in a box
Where it's dark all day
I have nothing to do here
Please take me away.

Sophie-Ann Walker (12)
Brooklands Middle School, Leighton Buzzard

Soldier At War

I'm a soldier
I sleep in a tree
When I walk out
I smell like pee

I walk down the road
Everyone can smell me
I saw a toad
No one adores me

I nearly got shot
It skimmed my shirt
My trousers got ripped
Now I have a skirt

No one hears me when I cry
When I'm alone I think I'm gonna die
Everyone hates me I barely get along
Ching ching ching all day long
Brrrrap!
Goodbye.

Liam Harmer (12)
Brooklands Middle School, Leighton Buzzard

21st Century Warfare

Mangled remains
Barbed wire stretches
Death toll rises
Gunfire's heard
As centurions fall
Gunners run
The sergeant signals
Retreat!

Jamie Stanton (12)
Brooklands Middle School, Leighton Buzzard

Night Sky

The night sky is a blanket tossed across the sun.
It's when the midnight glossy moon
is out of space and becomes Earth's light bulb.
As the wind swoops by
the autumn leaves walk along with the gravestones
guiding them to their lair as the midnight sky ends.

But when the clock hits 12 the world goes mad
as the disguised wolves come out
and the world turns into mayhem.
The cats go savage and the moonlight falls across the land
as the midnight hour ends.

James Quinn (10) & Nicky Walton (11)
Brooklands Middle School, Leighton Buzzard

Rubies

Rubies are a loving child,
Her eyes shining brightly.
Her smile cheers everyone up.
She brings baskets full of joy.
Her face shimmers in the sunlight.

Her magic circulates the dull world.
She never lets anyone be sad.
Her heart is full of happiness.
She just could explode.
Her magic changes the frowns
On other children's faces.
She is always happy.

Chloe Reid (10)
Brooklands Middle School, Leighton Buzzard

Global Warming

G lobal warming is a serious problem.
L ives of animals are dying
O r they are becoming extinct.
B ecause of ice caps melting,.
A n ice cap melts every day
L eaving only a few for animals to live

W hy is global warming happening
A nd what have done to deserve it?
R espect the world? We have not!
M aking more pollution from our cars.
 I don't think that is right.
N ever recycling, we have to cut more trees.
G oing to lose more ice caps. Animals are at risk.

Nastassja Squire (12)
Brooklands Middle School, Leighton Buzzard

Soldier Undercover

I'm a soldier undercover
I am missing my mother
There is not another day
That goes by when I'm not undercover.

There is not a day I'm not afraid
I am made to raid
So be afraid.

I'm a soldier undercover
I am missing my mother
There is not another day
That goes by when I'm not undercover.

Charlie Denham (13)
Brooklands Middle School, Leighton Buzzard

Homelessness

I'm sitting alone at the side of a path,
People walk by me and just stare and laugh.
As the cold of the winter slowly approaches
I seem to attract points from people on coaches.
Sometimes a pitying person may give me some food,
But others look at me, acting rather crude.
Children walk by, happy as a lark,
I hope they won't end up like me, sitting in the dark.
I don't want to die on these cold, lonely streets
But I just wish I had something good to eat.
Life on the streets isn't so great,
You're hungry and alone, without even a mate.
I regret my decisions, I regret my life
So I slowly lie down and reach for the knife.

Lucy Woods (12)
Brooklands Middle School, Leighton Buzzard

Pollution Poem - Haikus

People are so cruel
Little animals are dead
If we do not stop.

Aerosols in cans
Killing the ozone layer
We will all be burned.

If we don't stop soon
We will all be burnt right through
So please, please stop *now*.

Louise Docherty (11)
Brooklands Middle School, Leighton Buzzard

Alone

I am left here in the cold darkness
No one could love me now, I am a right mess
I was left to die
But what I can't understand is why?
It's help I need to seek
But I am just too weak
I need some help
But I can't even yelp
I am slipping from consciousness
My life is getting less and less
I know I will not see the light of day again
Or the wetness of the rain
I know this happens all over the world
Helpless animals being hurled
Into ditches, rubbish tips as well
For this is living hell
I wish they could feel what I feel now
They can do this but I don't know how
I feel sad and alone
I realise it is my turn to go.

Lewis Eykelbosch (11)
Brooklands Middle School, Leighton Buzzard

Soldiers At War

The muddy, bloody trenches.
The unbelievable stenches.
Soldiers stuck on barbwire fences.
I started shaking in fear
As my eyes shed a tear.
Then came all the deadly bombers
Shooting madly, we're all goners.
As I took my last deep breath
And then it's time for a gory death.

Luke Burroughes & Chris Bulpit (12)
Brooklands Middle School, Leighton Buzzard

Best Friends

B est friends forever we will be.
E ver and ever together are we.
S ecrets shared between us, no one will know.
T ogether we will stand, ready, get set and go.

F orever and ever we will be together.
R ather than fighting we are always there for each other.
I gnoring people who are mean to you,
   we will always stick together.
E ndless fun for everyone.
N ever step out of line.
D emand everything will be just fine.
S kipping with joy, we will be together forever.

Sarah Johnson (12), Olivia Cherry & Tierney Spence (11)
Brooklands Middle School, Leighton Buzzard

Split Ups

Always arguing, never stops
Lots of children
Crying, doesn't stop
Tell us to gather round
I find out the news
I fall to the ground
They're getting divorced
How did this happen?
My mum hit him with a batten
I feel so sorry
But we're all happy now
Me, my mum and brother
Just us three now.

Kayleigh Cawley (11)
Brooklands Middle School, Leighton Buzzard

Mums Are Great

My mum is great
let's all celebrate
from the day she was alive
she became full of life.

My mum is amazing
we're always debating,
'Who are you sitting next to today Mother?'
'I don't know, my brother?'

My mum is cool
she bought a pool
it's full of water
to make lots of laughter.

My mum is bright
there's no point having a fight
she'll always win
and give us a grin.

My mum is pretty
so don't be witty
she's the best mum on the dance floor
so men always knock on the door.

My mum is wicked
although she was kicked
she now has a cat
which she gives a good pat.

So let's all shout
because there's no doubt
mums are best
when they irons your vests.

Charlotte Drake & Kate Ellerton (11)
Brooklands Middle School, Leighton Buzzard

I'm A Soldier

I'm a soldier,
I live in a trench,
I'm nearly always
Sleeping on a bench.

I used to hide
In the trench at a side
In the grass
Where someone died.

I'm a soldier,
I live in a trench,
I'm nearly always
Sleeping on a bench.

I miss my friends
And seeing family at the weekend.
I miss them all,
All the family and friends.

I'm a soldier,
I live in a trench,
I'm nearly always
Sleeping on a bench.

I hunt, I have stunts,
I curl, I grunt
I watch the things
I shouldn't watch.

So don't come near
Or I will bite
Because there is lots of fights.

You don't want to be in a fight, fight,
I want to be free.

Shanice Morgan (12)
Brooklands Middle School, Leighton Buzzard

I Am A Soldier

I am a soldier
I live in a trench
I'm nearly always
Sleeping on a bench.

I miss my wife who's in my heart,
I miss my home-made jam tarts.

I dream, I cry
And I wave goodbye.

So don't come near
Or I will bite
Because there are lots and lots of fights,
Because I'm scared,
Can't you understand!

Victoria Krzywopulski (11)
Brooklands Middle School, Leighton Buzzard

World War I

Soldiers are great
Soldiers are strong
And nearly always
Singing sad songs.

Soldiers are hard
Soldiers are bad
And they're sometimes
Really sad.

They're scary
But they're great
And they are
An excellent mate.

Jedd Harding (11)
Brooklands Middle School, Leighton Buzzard

Criminals

The world is full of criminals, it's not safe anymore.
So many underage drinkers, trying to break the law.
So many young children, all alone.
There isn't a place they can call home.
They created Childline,
Did they think that would work?
If the parents found out, it would just give them a perk.

Drugs and drinking,
What are they thinking?
What's going through their mind?
Something must be confined.

Megan Davies & Paige Hales (11)
Brooklands Middle School, Leighton Buzzard

Shoes

So many shoes, but only two feet,
I wish that I could buy every pair that I meet,
They look so new and cool,
But on me they'll look like a fool,
Some are high heels that'll make me tall,
And some shoes that'll make me small,
Shoes come in all shapes and sizes,
And some shoes are low prices,
I wish that my feet were smaller,
That way I'll look much cooler,
As I'm a size bigger than I should be,
And that is the embarrassment for me!

Chelcie Page, Nicole Sellars & Charlotte Furie (11)
Brooklands Middle School, Leighton Buzzard

In Dreamland

When I sleep only you are in my thoughts,
My mind is racing when you're near me,
My heart pounds as I look into your eyes,
My passion for you is far better than another,
When I feel your soft touch upon my skin,
I know that you're the one for me,
My spirit and my heart are forever yours,
As your precious lips press upon my skin,
My love for you grows stronger than ever before,
I see roses blossoming above our heads,
I see our future for I know our love is crucial,
Our love will never end, till death is upon us,
If our hands touch one thing will lead to another.
When I feel your breath upon my face,
I want you to come closer to me,
I want to feel free with you for I can't with any other,
If only you were real and not just a ghostly figure in my dream!

Sharon Shumbambiri & Paige Archer (12)
Brooklands Middle School, Leighton Buzzard

They're Only Sick So Don't Take The Mick!

What happens to the people with no money,
Can't even afford a jar of honey?
Rain pouring over their heads,
Their daughter's died, their son is dead.

There is no food, the food is gone,
They have been starving all year long.
Chucked out onto the street,
Making shoes to protect their feet.
Stared at, glared at, when people walk by,
The old lady begins to cry.
Why does the world have to be so cruel?
The world's so big but it seems so small.

Lauren Elwood & Michelle Fenn (11)
Brooklands Middle School, Leighton Buzzard

Myths

Unicorn's eyes twinkle in the moonlight,
As she runs across the shimmering lake.
Sometimes disappearing during the night,
Making magic they start to ache.

Fairies playing in the sky,
As they flitter across the clouds.
They start to make magic,
Making wishes come true.

Mermaids swimming in the deep blue,
As they pass the gorgeous angelfish.
She flippers her tail that's new
As her merdad comes to give her a kiss.

Angels coming down from above,
Flying gracefully like a bluebird.
As they pass through good and bad times
They leave magic for the sick and hopeful.

Ashleigh Taylor & Natasha Cooper (10)
Brooklands Middle School, Leighton Buzzard

Brooklands Middle School

Brooklands rocks
The county thinks it sucks,
We have to stop the closure
Before Brooklands' history is over.

I think they've got it wrong
It will make the journey long,
They've made the biggest mistake of their lives.

They'll break my friendship
If they close this school
Brooklands is so cool,
The teachers at this school
They actually don't act like fools.

Rachel Chambers & Chloe Shadbolt (10)
Brooklands Middle School, Leighton Buzzard

Brooklands Middle School Closure

The classrooms and the cloakrooms galore,
Sun is shining bright and golden,
As the councillors announce the school might close,
Black heavy clouds rain upon our heads.

Friends being split up,
A lot of sorrow would come.
If they closed our school down,
In our hearts we're to sadden.

A funeral takes place,
As Brooklands is knocked down,
But if we change the council's mind,
Our school will stay open.

In our hearts the school shall be
Forever resting peacefully.
We will miss our funny school
When we're in upper school.

We'll fight for eternity,
To keep our school open for another day.

Isobel Winward & Caitlin Blair (10)
Brooklands Middle School, Leighton Buzzard

Living Alone

Sitting all cold, lonely and wet.
It's people like me that people forget.
I have no home, no friends, no car, no money.
People walk past me and find me funny.
At night when I'm walking to my old wooden bench
I'm scared someone's behind me so I begin to clench.
I wake up in the morning to find my money all gone.
I'm living a life that has all gone wrong.

Rebecca Mead & Lizzie Hawkins (12)
Brooklands Middle School, Leighton Buzzard

Welcome To The World Of Football

Fans - arriving
Floodlights - glowing
Stadium - buzzing
Whistle - blowing
Ball - swerving
Attackers - shooting
Defenders - blocking
Goalkeeper - catching
Legs - tiring
Harsh - tackling
Player - limping
Linesman - conferring
Red card - showing
Fans - booing
Managers - hollering
Penalty - taking
Minutes - ticking
Fans - anticipating
Hearts - pounding
Goal - scoring
Supporters - cheering
Scarves - waving.

Welcome to the world of . . . football.

Jamie Pender (11)
Challney High School for Boys, Luton

The Vicious Tsunami

Loud as an elephant,
Angry as a lion, it will destroy your house,
It is as sneaky as a mouse,
Gruesome as the bogeyman,
As strong as Goliath,
Quick as the wind,
It will always demolish all in its way.

Fazeel Talib (12)
Challney High School for Boys, Luton

Football Mad

Oh no! Bless my soul!
Clever Trevor's scored a goal!

So he runs up the pitch
And wriggles his botty
He is kissed by ten men
All sweaty and snotty.
Now he's waving his fist
To the Queen who just stares -
The lad's going crazy
But everyone cheers!
Now what's he doing?
He's chewing the cud!
He's rolling in the mud!
Now he's crying!
I think he's in pain.
Now what's he doing?
He's smiling again!

Oh no! Bless my soul!
Clever Trevor's scored a goal!

He's doing gymnastics
He's doing some mime
He's kissing the ground for a very long time
He's now on his back
With his feet in the air
Now he's gone all religious
And stopped for a prayer!
Did he pray for the sick?
Did he pray for the poor?
No, he prayed for the ball
And he prayed to score.
No one but no one
Can restart the game
Until Trevor has had
His moment of fame!

Oh no! Bless my soul!
Clever Trevor's scored a goal!
He kicked the ball into the net . . .
How much money will he get?

Ataf Arif (13)
Challney High School for Boys, Luton

Fireworks

Fireworks blast,
Fireworks pop!
Everyone loves them very much.
Different colours,
Indigo, violet,
Colours from the rainbow.
What would we do without them?
You blast on parties!
With a hot blazing light,
Lighting up the street!
Awakening the people asleep.

Umar Khan (11)
Challney High School for Boys, Luton

Miss Norie

My name is Corrie,
And this is the story,
Of my teacher, Miss Norie,
Hitting me and my friend Torrie.

She's actually supposed to teach me,
But instead she beats me,
She hasn't got a degree,
She smashed my head with a CD,
She likes to drink tea
But she's like a killer bee!

Arandeep Bains (13)
Challney High School for Boys, Luton

The Forest Of Midnight Darkness

In this dark, foreboding forest a man walks through.
A graveyard he sees before him
opening in-between the twisting, suffering trees.
He enters the holy resting place of the deceased,
dark demons of evil.
The gothic cathedral with the carvings of evil incarnate
plastered all over in choirs of darkness.
He was overwhelmed by the dark, phantom-like figures,
flying around the room.
He was never seen again . . .

Billy Saunders (13)
Challney High School for Boys, Luton

The Old Man - Haiku

With nothing to do,
Except smoke the cigarettes.
Death shall be coming.

Asim Iqbal (11)
Challney High School for Boys, Luton

My Generation

My generation is a teenage generation,
I am very quiet,
I love to watch TV
On a Saturday night
And sit in no light.

My favourite colour is purple,
I am very playful,
I like people to call me Playful Emz,
I love to hang with friends,
I am very careful.

Emma Wilson (13)
Hastingsbury School, Kempston

My Generation

My generation is full of bad things
Yobs hanging round with their guns, all you hear is *bang, bang!*
Police ring their doorbell,
'Sorry he's dead.'
Good things do happen . . .
Like children growing up, shopping, cinemas
And parties all night long.
Teenagers are independent, they don't want parents around.
Fashion conscious and going up town.
My generation is wonderful but depressing.

Stacey Garner (13)
Hastingsbury School, Kempston

Untitled

Our life is full of a lot of things
Yes, it is about boys and bling.

Italian boys are who we like best.
They've got that six-pack under their vests.
Boy crazy, boy mad
Now we've just got to add that sexy Italian flag.

We want to be famous together
Because we know our love will last forever.

We can't forget about those boys we have hurt
But you can't blame us for being flirts!

Selina Bri-ana, Abbie Roberts & Louise Peacock (13)
Hastingsbury School, Kempston

Today's Generation

Nowadays the parents just don't understand
They don't get our flow, the way we rollin' round
They sit and tell us about back in the day
The way we now hang but they used to 'play'.

Complaining we're always staying out late
Feeding us the food we really hate
No ganging and hanging in the street
People aren't the same like we used to meet.

They try to take us out with them
When we want to be out with our friends
Get home from school, no hanging about
Keep your trap shut, there's no need to shout.

They really know the ways to annoy us
Always moaning and making a fuss
They complain about the music we listen to
They just don't know what's the new.

Change your clothes and brush your hair
They go on like an endless nightmare
Clean your room, sort out that mess
You sit doing nothing, you're so useless.

They go on talking 'bout their penny sweets
Now they complain about McDonald's we eat
Grans come and drown us with a kiss
Knitting us jumpers not on our Christmas list!

We don't want to be doing household chores
Those are the things we find a bore
Give us time, have some patience
You don't understand, we're today's generation!

Priya Kumari (14)
Hastingsbury School, Kempston

My Generation

Bang, bang, the sound of guns,
every night down the alley.
A whiff of smoke,
from the weed smokers in massive groups.
Mobiles going off
and giggling girls reading their texts from their boyfriends.
Young children riding down the street,
being watched by paedophiles.
Drugs and alcohol,
being taken by everyone.
Old English, to new English, to slang,
'Thee, the', then 'da . . .'
Schools aren't as strict,
but the law is.
'Mum!' the next-door neighbours hear.
'Lemme a tenna!
I'm goin' into town,
So I need money but I'm skint!'
Music has changed.
In *your* days it was classical.
It isn't no more!
As you see,
our generation is a lot different to yours.
Now let us be
and now it's time to close some doors.

Katie Payne (13)
Hastingsbury School, Kempston

My Generation

My generation has changed through the years
It is now full of yobs
And people full of fear.

kids are in detention for being late to class,
And forgetting their homework,
How long will this last?

Teenagers who are walking around in gangs,
People getting shot,
The world full of bangs.

Underage girls are getting pregnant,
Lads only wanting one thing,
The parents are negligent.

Smoking and drinking, an unhealthy world,
Obese children,
Chips - straight or curled.

But not all is bad, some is good,
Most people live happily,
Like we all should.

The families are together, eating healthy food,
Laughing and smiling,
No one is rude.

This is my generation, good and bad,
Some are happy, some are sad,
Some are rich, some are poor,
Some are at peace, some are at war.

Abigail Williamson (14)
Hastingsbury School, Kempston

One Girl, One World

She sits beneath her window
Tears rolling down her face,
Pouring her heart out,
At an alarming pace.

Why she cries
She does not know.
All of these problems
Are making her feel low.

People don't seem to listen,
So she writes her feelings on paper,
Doesn't think of the consequences -
Of what might bring later.

She loves to write
She loves to draw,
But with her tears
The rain outside pours.

As the poems increase,
They're something to talk to,
To try and prevent the pain
That she's been going through.

When people see her poems
They think it's depression,
But they don't know
That she uses it as an expression.

An expression of her feelings,
Of what she feels inside,
At the moment all feelings of happiness
Have just gone and just died.

Kirsty McCulley (14)
Hastingsbury School, Kempston

My Generation

M y generation nowadays is full of
Y oung, youthful people, some are

G enerous whilst others are not,
E ven though they've got everything they want
N obody seems to be happy,
E very day there is at least one murder,
R obbers and gun crime,
A re more and more.
T exting, internet and emails,
I s all they seem to be interested in.
O n a positive note schools are less strict,
N owadays are the days some people dread whilst others love.

Jodie Worrall (13)
Hastingsbury School, Kempston

My Generation

M y generation
Y oung children getting hurt and stabbed.

G oing out clubbing and having fun,
E nergy turning to being glum,
N ever going without their phones,
E arning money to spend on clothes,
R emembering the days when we were poor
A ll nowadays kids can only think of 'more!'
T eachers teaching kids who can't be bothered,
I ndoors children don't act themselves, 'til they get
O utdoors to get their freedom to smoke
and drink and break the law,
N ow young ones are acting like olders
and leaving their childhood behind.

Rhonica McGillvary (13)
Hastingsbury School, Kempston

Blue Eyes

Through your lovely blue eyes, I know what you think and want
Your eyes are the gateway to your soul and your heart
Through your eyes I see you try to fight the love that hurts you
My arrows of love will touch your heart shaped like a dartboard.

The love I hold for you will not escape as long as you don't try
to break my heart
Through the eyes I see your love but you push me and hurt me
The day we met my love was strong, but now my love turns to hate
The sweetness of your heart tries to break through to tell me,
But one day you will tell me.

Weeks we were apart but all I could think about was you
and your eyes,
Through your angel blue eyes I could stare in them forever
and get lost,
You wait too long and my love will slowly die
Through the year I try so hard to keep my love or it will
forever be lost.

Kaya Lightfoot (14)
Hastingsbury School, Kempston

My Generation

My name is Steph, I love to go shopping
Whatever me and my buddies do it's always popping
I smile and laugh every day
My life is fabulous and hot in every way
I look on the bright side
And hold my head up with pride
Me and my buddies are always chatting
And always know what is happening
I'm like a little Barbie, I love pink
And I'm totally girly, don't you think?

Steph Wiggins (14)
Hastingsbury School, Kempston

Fighting

I hate people who fight,
People fight in front of me,
People fight behind me,
People try and curse me.

I hate people who fight,
They all punch and slap,
But they all seem big and tough,
People try and curse me.

I hate people who fight,
People who fight make me sick,
People use weapons like stones and sticks,
People try and curse me.

I hate people who fight,
They make themselves look big,
I will hit if people hit me,
People try and curse me.

Charlotte Brassington (14)
Hastingsbury School, Kempston

Friends

Friends are there
They do not envy

Friends are trustworthy
Friends are a blanket

Friends are your shield
They are your light

Friends feel your void
Without friends I would not be the same.

Conor Smith (15)
Hastingsbury School, Kempston

My Generation

My generation,
are all so very young,
we love to go to parties,
we live to have fun.

My generation,
are full of emos, chavs and goths,
they all seem to hate each other,
I just like the lot.

My generation,
all seem to love to fight,
on the outside they act all dumb,
but inside they're really bright.

Zoe Mason (14)
Hastingsbury School, Kempston

My Generation

I'm a shopaholic
So I love spending money,
I'm a chocoholic,
So I love chocolate in my tummy.

I enjoy going on MSN
And chatting to my mates,
I like boys not men,
Who takes me on dates.

I'm such a bubbly chick
Who loves to smile,
I'm good at athletics
And love to run a mile.

Charlotte Lenton (14)
Hastingsbury School, Kempston

Teenagers:
Are We All As Bad As People Think?

Most teenagers are good,
Most teenagers are great,
So why do people think they *all* intimidate?

The vandalism, the smoking and all of that,
Are only done by the teenagers that show off
And that's a fact.

The big groups and gangs make people scared,
But what are we doing wrong?
Nothing, that's what's weird.

Threatening, harassing, that's not all teenagers' thing,
But we all get the blame for harassment and threatening.

They say you shouldn't judge a book by its cover,
But we're judged without knowing because we're teenagers.

Most teenagers scream and say, 'It's not fair,'
But if you think about it,
Is *this* really fair?

Prabjoth Kaur (14)
Hastingsbury School, Kempston

My Generation

The generation of youths, yobs, young hooligans,
But we're not all like that, it's just a small few of 'em.
They run the streets like maniacs, psychotics,
Get stuck down your throat like a pack of throat Lockets.
It ain't all of us though, but it sure feels like it,
Opening the paper, 'Teenagers again at it'.
But now I'm here, I can't change my generation,
Just gotta get on with it, like the rest of the nation.

Sonia Sandhu (13)
Hastingsbury School, Kempston

Not All Bad

Late night parties
Drinking 'til seven
Short, short skirts
Seven minutes in Heaven

Glossy lips ready to kiss
Foundation really thick
Blusher on the cheeks
Thick, thick eyeliner making them peek

1 in the morning seems like 11
Standing outside Best One
Smoking whatever

But not all teenagers are like this
Maybe one in seven
So don't think we are, you see
Most of our bedtimes are 7.

Amy-Kate Cleary (13)
Hastingsbury School, Kempston

My Generation

M others crying
Y oung children dying

G randads mugged
E veryone's a thug
N o one's happy
E motions are snappy
R apists killing
A ngry mobs milling
T raffic wardens billing
I nfants are thrilling
O pen minds chilling
N *ot my generation!*

Bethany Smith (13)
Hastingsbury School, Kempston

My Generation

At 14 I am different to my parents
I go out with my friends
My mum goes to work
But I don't want to.
I want to go on MSN but I have to help
I run around like a child
And I care about the way I look
And I don't like reading books
I go on Bebo, My Space and Face Book.
Look at my friends
And remember the good times.
My grandparents don't want to know about what I get up to
Telling me stories of what they used to do
Wars and rationing
I would not survive
I wouldn't like to live in 1865.
No computers, no make-up
I don't know if I want to wake up
Bebo I love
My family always going on about life
And what I'm going to make of it.

Abi Sweeney (14)
Hastingsbury School, Kempston

My Generation

Two generations
One the eldest
One the younger
The eldest wise
The youngest foolish
One under pressure
One with no clue
One rejected
One accepted
But both united.

Eleanor Bates (13)
Hastingsbury School, Kempston

Just A Girl

She's just a girl that's all she is
all day she stands alone.
In a crowded playground
with no company but her own.

Her make-up's smudged
from recent tears
from all her dreams,
her hopes and fears.

Each day she faces more torment
her parents will never know
the dreaded place called school,
but she knows she has to go.

'It won't go on forever,'
is what she tells herself
and soon will be her birthday,
this will be her twelfth.

Another year has passed her by
some things she won't forget,
one thing that will stay forever
is the day she and her bullies met.

Chelsey Hancock (14)
Hastingsbury School, Kempston

A Dark Background

The day I was born
For my mother I did mourn
She brought me here but not everything is clear
And from that day pain was always in the way
Preventing me from what I want to be.

People on the street walk past and peer
They laugh at me, point and jeer
Looking at this dreadful face of mine
But I have to pretend it's fine.

I lower my head and wish I was dead
Still they don't understand why
These scars on my face are a big disgrace
That were given to me by my mum.

She didn't die and go into the sky.
She pulled out her knife and then
She slashed away all day and night
Intent on killing this child before her.

But when I didn't die and lay there sleeping
She turned the knife upon herself
There was a gleam of light and a scream of fright
And there she was lying on the floor.

So I skulk about the shadows
Covering my face, not wanting people to see
What damage a mother could do to her child
Is there any point of life for me?

I walk down a road and a bottle lies there
I pick it up and smash it on the wall
I look up to the sky bright blue
And wish that wherever I go I'm with you.

Sophie Phillips (14)
Lealands High School, Luton

See

My eyes did see the same as you,
Colours gold, green, red and blue
Till the day cancer came to call,
Now my eyes don't see at all.

A world of darkness for a boy who cannot see,
No handicap school or white cane for me.
I do know now that I must fight -
I need to see but not with sight.

No time for self-pity, no time to waste,
Sight is important, I need it post haste.
I discovered I 'click' and the sound comes back to me.
Could I develop this method so that I can see?

I have a tongue and I have two ears,
Sight and sound have gone together for years.
If I can click and the sound waves come back,
I can learn if things are round or if they are flat.

At last I find a new way to see.
Crossing the road - it's not hard for me.
All I do is click to find my way.
Doctors are still baffled to this day.

No supersonic hearing have I,
No self-pity, no wanting to die.
For, with a click, I now can see
The world that is beautiful all around me.

Danielle Benson (14)
Lealands High School, Luton

Darkness Is Within Us

D oes one exist without meaning?
A re we all put here for nothing?
R ight above our heads, God laughs at us.
K een to be real, I search for meaning.
N o, for myself. But where do I start?
E xtend my arms towards space, to move the moon and stars?
S earch the galaxy for God or any type of higher power?
S hould I even take my own life in order to meet Him?

I s there really any God to begin with?
S hould I just look for seclusion from life?

W ithin myself, I see no soul, no heart, and no love.
I 'm nothing, but do we all feel this?
T he pain of being no one to anyone?
H ow do I know if others are truly being loved or in love?
I nside them is probably the same feeling that is inside me.
N ow that I know the truth, I shall not succumb to this higher power.

U nder my skin may be physical matter, but no spiritual essence.
S hall I merely surrender to the darkness?
    The same darkness that is within all of us?

Sanjay Pattani (14)
Lealands High School, Luton

Why Me?

I grew up a happy child,
A happy, carefree child.
Mother, Father,
Brothers and sisters.
But all that changed . . .

No one expects it to happen to them.
I was one of them.
But one day,
That dreadful day,
Everything changed.

It tears me apart.
I wake up in the morning, contemplating my life.
'How long do I have left?'
'How is my body coping?'
Everything is changing.

But here I am,
One year on.
Still fighting,
Still hoping,
Still praying,
Still alive.

Jenna Kay (15)
Lealands High School, Luton

Grief, Sadness, Despair

Beautiful, blonde and sleek,
Beauty of which no one can speak,
Her eyes as blue as the ocean wide,
Elegance calls with every stride.
But behind her eyes there is pain,
Grief, sadness and despair.
There is no one who did care.
Her true face hidden behind a mask,
Hiding that face is her lifelong task.
Behind that mask, if someone was to see,
No longer is what her life would be.
Grief, sadness and despair tenfold,
There is no one who does care.

Joshua Denham (14)
Lealands High School, Luton

Love

Love is a word, a word of deep meaning,
No one can describe love,
To me love lies deep at the bottom of your heart,
However, how does it all start?
Your heart is there to help you decide whom you love,
Like an angel that one special person is above,
Waiting for you to say those three special words . . .
'I love you.'

Shaan Sagoo (14)
Lealands High School, Luton

Insomniac

In a bit of light I stay awake
This bit of light's my hope.
In the dark I await my fears
With dark I just can't cope.

I close my eyes and darkness comes
Draining out all light.
This is why I stay awake
It's better than dreaming in fright.

Night after night I lie awake
My eyes itching to close.
But stubbornly I keep opening my eyes
As fear will come if I doze.

If only I could dream of dreary daisies
Of a world full of cheers
But I lie awake at night
Because I dream only of my fears.

The light - my hope - keeps me awake
I clutch to it despite
It keeps me up, wide awake
Which screws me up inside.

This lack of sleep brings home: the madness,
Red eyes, shortness of delight,
Light, keeps away the darkness
That so riddles me with fright.

Konica Jamal (16)
Luton Sixth Form College, Luton

You Know Everything

You know everything about us, but what do we know about you?
We might glimpse in the glimmer of the moonlight,
Or a fall of dappled light,
You might speak in the rustle of a leaf or a whisper of a breeze,
But what message do you speak, if you speak at all?
You live to raise the ones who are down, catch those who fall,
But if you write the script then why all the troublemakers?

How does it feel to be so high?
To feel the softness of the clouds - the innocence of the world
Do you cry when the ones you love and care for are down?
Do you feel our pain by walking in our shoes?

Do you send the happiness and love we crave so much?
Like the pure white dove flying over the trees,
Gazing down at its lower world,
Have you ever felt starved? Ever felt full?
Filled with the love of the world
How do you decide our fates
If they are already wrapped around your finger?

You blow like the wind, shine like the stars,
You are forever there when we are done, done with life,
And you raise us up, to be whole, to be one, to be part of you,
For you to be part of us.

So tell me why I feel so far away, when you're so close?
I can feel you changing sadness to joy,
Fears to hopes, my dreams to plans
Have I missed my chance, a chance to be whole with you?
All I wanted to do was to dance,
Dance in the moonlight, dance to the stars
Your stars, the ones you created,
The ones that shine as bright as you.

So how does it feel to be so high?
When you look down at us, do you feel happy or do you feel sad?

So when the light slips around the ageless trees
And the shadows dance on a whispering breeze
Allow us to discover magic, the magic of knowing you
And knowing you love the world for who we are.

Becky Dunne (16)
Luton Sixth Form College, Luton

Waking Up At Sunset

Sunday again, I arise . . .
With white eyeliner around my eyes.
I look in the mirror, who do I see?
Nothing but a blemish on society.

Monday through Friday, I am forced to place . . .
This disgusting optimistic smile on my face.
Gifted and blessed, I break every stereotype rule!
I didn't think the ticket to Heaven was to be cool.

Me, a black female that dances to hard rock . . .
In that hard place is my battle around the clock.
Is it a crime, to have a different beat to chime?
You poison my lacerations with your bitter limes.

That adoring yellow rose, you crushed like a toxin . . .
Accompanied by the orange in which you stripped away the skin.
You cracked the red whip, for your own adulterated pleasure!
Deep purple ink is worthless and goes without measure.

Saturday night, a velvet blanket at twilight . . .
However no stars are reflected in my sight.
A new day tomorrow, why should I miss out on God's blessing?
Because I wish to rise while the sun is setting.

Whilst dreaming, I am free to be who I am destined to be . . .
So I wake up at sunset like shadows behind a tree.
Uninhabited and confident, why should I give a single damn!
Yet foolishly I still wonder . . . why can't you accept me for who I am?

Loess-Rose Mills (16)
Luton Sixth Form College, Luton

Today's Women From A Woman's Perspective

It's like intelligence, you either got it or you don't,
It's the same with morals, you either use them or you won't,
The crazy thing today isn't the youth of today,
But the women of today,
Now speaking from a woman's perspective,
The only thing that is expected,
Is pure honesty and facts,
Because you girls are beginning to prove the stats,
And it just isn't right, why is it some of you just can't say no,
Letting a man make a joke out of you to then not want to know?
Once upon a time you women would have stood your ground,
But now the majority of you are just getting around,
If you girls continue to carry on this way,
Our younger generation will then think it's OK,
To imitate the same antics as you do,
Not caring of the consequences that will soon come through.

Girls we need to stick together, what happened to girl power?
Well that knowledge is decreasing by the hour,
We can't be letting the male species get the better of us,
They might think using us is OK then they look at us in disgust,
As though it doesn't take two to tango and it's entirely our doing,
And this kind of analogy is what keeps intruding,
Upon our own initiative and women's intuition,
Come on girls, there's more to life than this, explore your ambitions,
Make something of your lives, stop with the thoughtless actions,
And you'll find things will get better
And there'll be fewer complications.

Now in case you're getting it twisted, I'm one who acts differently,
I keep my goodies for the special one that has respect for me,
The way I see it is, God put us on the Earth to reproduce,
Not to abuse the gift and go about acting loose,
Our bodies are precious and shouldn't be exposed to just any man,
If so respect is lost and there'll be nothing to stop you
From losing stand,
I respect myself because my body is my temple,
If I don't neither will anyone else and I need to set an example,
For other girls just like myself and more,
Who are strong and independent
With something to offer the world in store.
To be honest I don't care what other girls choose to do
With their time,
I make my own decisions on what I do with mine,
If no pride is shown throughout the women of the majority,
I would therefore prefer to be my own person
As part of the minority . . .

Michaela Penny (17)
Luton Sixth Form College, Luton

Everything For Me Is Free

I don't pay no mortgage
I don't pay no rent
I don't get gas or electric bills
They don't get sent

I don't pay council tax
I don't pay for my food
Some people can't pay their bills
Then they worry and brood

I live in a house
I sleep anywhere
Sometimes I have mates in
Everything we share

I watch the telly
Listen to the radio
People come in the house
They come and go

Sometimes people try to kill me
I usually get away
If it gets too bad
In the house I don't stay

I go to another house
I can live where it suits me
I don't go to work
Because everything for me is free

I don't eat a lot
I am very small
Everyone has seen me
I am the fly on the wall.

Yeliz Tacel (16)
Luton Sixth Form College, Luton

My Generation

Mobile phone pressed to my ear
Supposed to be private, but all can hear
Congregating on street corners
Meeting friends, making plans.

Make-up, fashion
All made to look good
But if only people understood
We wear hair up, wear hair down
Coloured, curled, combed
It's up to us.

Don't make a fuss
My generation does care
Give us the chance to show you
It's you only being fair.

We'll take our place in society
Not to face your condemnation
But give us a chance for laughter
A happy life is all we're after.

We are good. My generation.

Chelsea Robson (12)
Neale Wade Community College, March

Rapstars Roll

I roll in a car
In a Jaguar
I'm singing a song
All night long
I've got big ass rims
Drinking those Pimms.

I'm on the road
Here I go
My name is Joe
The coppers, they know.

Joe Lilley (13)
Neale Wade Community College, March

The Fate Of Immortal Solitude, Trapped In An Endless Reality

Had 'Solitude' as his acquired name,
As he was once the solitude itself.
His life preceding was there to blame,
Filled with desires to be immortal.

Came to an ending - his first false fake life.
He arrived to and conquered the heavens -
Adam's apples were chopped apart in half,
And his lusts were fulfilled in the twilight.

At the sunrise the offers were flying,
Getting closer towards him, like flashlights
Of a car in destruction destroying . . .
'Forget all your sins, accept to go back

As today's realised incarnation
Of the actual Solitude - be it.
Then pursue those deserving frustration -
Feeling framed by a lonely illusion.'

Second life. Second chance. He had wondered
Why all those, who by loneliness condemned,
Were just walking. In sunsets. In hundreds.
Couldn't reach one another, like streetlights
Trapped in hopeless pain.

His eyes beautiful,
Shining lively, with useless, pointless thoughts
- Why did he have to paint those pictures
In the frames of false feelings, and fake noughts?
His blue hair, like night - apathetic -

Just like him. He had had enough of it all.
Could he try to escape from the stage like the wind?
From same streets surrounding him, and maybe fall
Again into a trap - off a cliff - with a grin.

Olga Shipunova (16)
Neale Wade Community College, March

My Generation

When I'm older,
I will fall in love,
With a man who has seen the galaxy,
Through time and space,
Who has seen Shakespeare.

I travel to save him and his friends,
They want to leave,
I'm trying to find,
To find pieces of a puzzle.

I tell a story,
Of a great man,
A man who has saved us so many times,
You don't know,
Without him,
History will take over.

I am searching alone,
With *no one,*
I have told a story,
To many people,
All over the world.

These people are to think,
To think of one word,
At one time,
To save the man who is trapped,
Trapped in time,
But that one word,
Will set him free.

Amy Martin (13)
Neale Wade Community College, March

All My Great Excuses

I started on my homework,
but my pen ran out.
My hamster ate my homework,
my computer's on the blink.

I accidentally dropped it
in the soup my mum was cooking.
My brother flushed it down the toilet,
when I wasn't looking.

'It rained on the way to school today,'
I said to the teacher with doubt.
He said, 'I don't believe you Laura.'
I replied, 'Fine, I'll scream and shout.'

I don't see why they won't agree,
I always get detention.
I'm a very convincing person you see,
It makes me very angry.

Laura Thornton (13)
Neale Wade Community College, March

School Chair

Lonely in school, in the summer holidays.
Day by day, they fly away.
Getting sat on, it's not very nice.
Chewing gum and loads of bums.
Hot in summer and cold in winter.
Dark at nights and hot in the day.
Things in my life are very grey.
Life as a chair . . .
Someday I hope someone will actually care.

Deniz Dalsar (12)
Neale Wade Community College, March

My Generation

My world
My generation is really quite bad,
there's people in the world who are very sad.

People live in houses,
people live in sheds,
some people don't even have a comfy bed.

Global warming
Global warming is wrecking our world,
the trees are dying and getting curled.

The planet is getting really hot,
it needs to cool down quite a lot.

If we don't take action very soon
it will be too late,
we'll have to live on the moon!

Robbie Coles (12)
Neale Wade Community College, March

My Generation

Chomping away on the grass all day,
Staying in my stable eating clumps of hay,
My hooves go *clipperty-clop,*
Oh my, I don't want to stop.

Getting a lot of attention from my human friends,
Hopefully my riding never ends,
Getting groomed then and again,
Having my hooves picked out is a pain.

But I love my rides and my stays,
And, I love my jumps and my plays.

Niomi Stromberg (12)
Neale Wade Community College, March

Abandoned . . .

Here I am in the cold
I'm not young but not that old
The twinkle's gone from in my eyes
All I see is dark grey skies.
My home is a broken box
My face looks like a fox
I eat old bones
And people moan
I don't like it, but I'll have to fight it.

My life is like a circle
With no beginning and no end
I have nobody, I need a friend
My box is in an alleyway
So dark and dingy, no hip or hooray
When I go to bed
Rain drips on my head
As my box is now soggy
Please help me, I'm only a doggy.

Charlotte Briley (12)
Neale Wade Community College, March

A Racer's Story

Vroom, vroom, rumble, puff,
I just can't get enough.
Speeding down that big ol' straight,
I honestly can't wait.

Burning round the track,
I don't bother looking back.
200 miles per hour,
I make other racers cower.

Luke Bancroft (13)
Neale Wade Community College, March

The World We Live In

The world nowadays, is not fair,
People never stop to take note or care,
All they do is pollute and destroy.

Some people take their time to care,
But others come to ruin it all,
They kill and swear and do not care.

People work hard for a good life,
But others come to ruin it all,
They do not care at their hard work,
They just care how much they steal.

You have feelings, emotions, thoughts and a unique style,
They come and laugh at who you are,
You say to them you do not care,
But deep inside it really hurts,
You're tired of racism, stereotyping and labelling,
But they just walk away without a care.

They know these actions keep you hurt,
But all you do is stay oblivious to their existence,
And plan a life without their kind,
Your heart still burns with hurt and hatred,
But you know you are the better person.

Daniel Tetnowski (12)
Neale Wade Community College, March

The Future

The future is unpredictable, with flying cars and gadgets.
You can change the future with ease
Opening doors with your keys.
With a touch of a button your life is rewritten,
Changing the world with your mittens.

Kirby Parrish (12)
Neale Wade Community College, March

Only A Day At School

When I wake up in the morning
I get ready for my shower
I bathe quietly while singing
But after an hour
I get ready for my grooming
My make-up's all set
It's ready for me
To pick it up quickly
Before it gets wet.

I'm ready for school
Jump onto the bus
My seat's already taken
I sit in the middle
Squashed up to my friends
The bus starts to move here and there
I hear the squeaks
And even the creaks
The bus finally stops
I quickly get off as I am in a puddle
I run to my locker
I shove my stuff in
I walk with my mate
Nice and cool
We wait outside the classroom
Waiting for the bell.

Ding-a-ling-ling
It finally goes
We run inside
And take a seat
Get down the objective
Don't forget the title
Now here comes the class
So here we go again
It's just another day at school
For me and my old joe.

Thank you God
For it's the end of the day
I go to my locker
And get my stuff out
I walk very slowly
Towards my bus I go
I sit down at the bottom
For I've got no energy left
School really tires you out
But it is the best.

The bus takes me home
I collapse on my bed
While getting some fruit
I turn on the music
Then go up to my room
For a quiet little snooze.

Anna Chesnaye (13)
Neale Wade Community College, March

Talkin' 'Bout My Generation

Life?

What
Is life?
Why
Are we here?
When
Do we leave this place?
Where
Do we go when our time is up?
How
Do we know we are real?
Life is a journey of confusion
Or is life a matter of dillusion?

Josh Middleton (12)
Neale Wade Community College, March

What Am I?

I am brown and white,
I have four feet,
I have a mane and tail,
What am I?

I am green and slimy,
I have four legs,
I live in a pond,
What am I?

I am fluffy,
I have four feet,
I go for walks,
What am I?

I have two fluffy ears,
I purr a lot,
I like being cuddled,
What am I?

Imogen James (13)
Neale Wade Community College, March

Life Of A Dog . . .

Sleeping and eating, that's all I do
Sitting in the corner chewing on someone's shoe
Lazing about on a summer's day
'Here boy, good boy,' as my owner would say.

Going for walkies is my favourite treat
Biscuits are my favourite thing I like to eat
Ice-cold water splashes on my face
Sometimes home is a lonely place.

I have lots of friends, mostly other dogs
Sometimes me and my owner go for jogs
Chasing cats, I think I might
But now I'm going to have a nap, goodnight.

Amber Cook (12)
Neale Wade Community College, March

My Generation

When I am older I would like to be a business lady.
I would like a mansion with a swimming pool.
In my house I would like a cinema, a private lake, a dance floor.
I would also like a Range Rover Sport,
Ferrari, Porsche and Lamborghini.

I would have my oldest family, like my mum and dad in a home.
I would get a car for my mum but she wouldn't drive it
        'cause she would be too old.
I would also have my own nightclub called Pinkies
With pink outside and inside.

I would also like to be rich.
I would have a good-looking boyfriend or husband.
I would probably have three home cinemas and 20 bedrooms.

Chloé Cooper-Watts (12)
Neale Wade Community College, March

Missing You Already

I know that this sounds stupid
And I know that there's no guy called Cupid
But I'm missing you already
So just promise me one thing, you'll take things steady
Soon I'm going to be hugging my teddy.
But honey, when you leave
I don't know whether I will breathe
I haven't known you for long
But I know your song
You've really made me think
You'll be gone in a blink.
Make sure you go steady
Because I'm missing you already.

Francesca Jeynes (12)
Neale Wade Community College, March

Talkin' 'Bout My Generation

My dog ate my homework
he got kicked out
I went to school with no homework
the teacher did scream and shout.

I got some more homework
my pencil snapped
then I couldn't do my homework
had to check the town map.

It started to rain on the way to town
everyone was inside the shops
I went inside a shop that wasn't full
I fell into a mop.

It finally stopped raining
I bought a silver pencil
I went back home to do my homework
then I needed a stencil.

I went into the kitchen
I got a pretty pink stencil
I went to do my homework
with my silver pencil.

Simone Demetriou (12)
Neale Wade Community College, March

Billy's True Story

I was born in a stable
but only stayed one day
a farmer came to get us
when we got there we played.

I found out where we were
we were on a farm
I was bred for meat
I was very alarmed.

A girl came to save me
she took me home
there were animals all round me
I was not alone.

I met a horse
and another baby goat
I was called Billy
she was just Goat.

They fed me with bottles
took me for walks
I was very happy
and the human even talks!

Emily Lunny (12)
Neale Wade Community College, March

Talkin' 'Bout My Generation

I hang on the field
Even though it is a wheel
So we go round and round
Until we are sick
And then I pick and flick
Until a headache appears.

I go home to a nag
When my brother comes home
And all he has is a bag
And I go to roam about the house.

When Mum comes home
All she does is sleep
Gets up and eats
And then more sleeping.

I miss my old primary school
I go to a bigger school now
You could get lost quite a few times
Teachers nag loads at uniform
But most people don't listen
Boring lessons, more boring
English is fun, maths is OK, science is boring.

Charlotte Field (12)
Neale Wade Community College, March

Talkin' 'Bout The Animals

Does my generation care
about the lost animals lying there?
Not getting lots of food and water
they're longing for some care
but this latest generation
don't seem to care.

Talkin' 'bout my generation,
they don't seem to care.
If only they knew
what the animals go through!

Just give them some love,
even just a hug.
All they want is a home
and a family who care!
Someone who will brush their hair.

Talkin' 'bout my generation,
all they do is play.
They never care
about the animals lying there,
so please care,
this generation,
it won't cost you at all!

Alexander King (12)
Neale Wade Community College, March

When The Owners Aren't There

Not again, the second time today.
They wouldn't be going if I had my say.
Well I'll make the most of it, I'll have some fun.
I'll go outside and have some fun in the sun.
I'll bark and growl as much as I want.

I'll chase my tail and jump about.
There's nobody here to scream and shout.
I'll fetch a stick, I'll chase a bee.
There's no one here who will see.
I'll roll in the mud and no one will know.

Oh no, they're here, they're coming through the door.
Anything I've done I hope no one saw.
They will think I've been asleep all day
When I've really been outside to play.
I can't wait until tomorrow.

I'll go and greet them at the door.
I bet they won't leave the door open anymore.
But all they care about is the cats on the bed.
They haven't noticed the mud (well they haven't said!).
I hope it's sunny tomorrow.

Bethany Darville (12)
Neale Wade Community College, March

My Typical Days At Home

I go to school and come home and I am not alone
My brother's there to give me a scare.
My typical days at home.

I do my homework to get it done
It's so boring I want to go out with my mates and have some fun.
My typical days at home.

I have my tea and watch a bit of TV
I go in my room and text on my phone.
My typical days at home.

It's 7pm, I have a bar of chocolate
I go on MSN and talk to Jordan and Abi, my friends.
My typical days at home.

I come off MSN and go in my room
Listen to Angels and Airwaves and Blink 182
And then I switch on the TV to see what's on ITV.
My typical days at home.

I brush my teeth and go to bed to rest my head.
My typical days at home.

Megan Pope (12)
Neale Wade Community College, March

The Generation

T eachers standing in the classroom
H aving nothing to do
E very day at the start of school

G oing to school at 8.30am
E njoying some lessons
N ever staying quiet
E veryone is fidgety
R atio, graphs in maths
A lso poetry in English
T urning the pencil round on the paper
I find some lessons boring
O n the paper we write
N ever-ending noise and chatter.

I n school still writing
N oise is all I can hear.

M y head is starting to ache.
Y es I want food when I get home.

L ying down on the sofa watching TV.
I n the fridge it's a cold blast
F rom 3.20pm till 10pm is relaxing time
E njoying time at home.

Hannah Taylor (12)
Neale Wade Community College, March

My Generation

Bell goes
Early alarm
I walk round school to find my mates
When I've found them we mess about round school.

Next bell
Get to the lockers
I wait till the last minute to put my bag away
So I have more time to mess about.

Late bell
Oh great
First lesson has started
How wonderful.

Lunch bell
Yippee
Time to go to the locker
And get my lunch out.

Last bell of the day
Yes, yes, yes
The bell has gone
So now we can all go home.

Sam Hall (12)
Neale Wade Community College, March

No More

Poverty in Africa far away
No more
Children starving far away
No more
People poor in the world far away
No more

War and fights far away
No more
Guns and shields far away
No more
Dead or alive far away
No more

Melting in the ice lands far away
No more
Animals die out far away
No more
Trees going chop far away
No more

We can't do anything far away.

Jordan Milnthorpe (12)
Neale Wade Community College, March

Talkin' 'Bout My Generation

Working all day
Working up and down
Splodging and splatting
What am I now?

As the bell rings
I'm ready to work again
Scratching and splatting
I'm like a hungry hen.

I'm put away in the pocket
All dark and cold inside
No more work today
I felt I'd almost died.

Another day on the paper
It's very hard you know
But sometimes you've got to deal with it
So let's go, go, go.

Katie Clements (12)
Neale Wade Community College, March

My Generation

I am Harry, I am twelve,
I am staring at the endless shelves,
Stacked high with new releases,
Thinking which one would please me,
My hand falls on one,
The new Fifa '08,
Great!
At home now,
One minute and I'll know how
To be the best I can.
Slide tackle,
To the left, to the right,
I can hear the fans cheering,
I am on the ball, it's me,
I am winning, easy for me,
I run past everyone,
I see my chance,
Shoot!
The fans roar,
Around the world, it's me they cheer for.

Harry Yardy (12)
Neale Wade Community College, March

My Generation

My generation,
My generation is very important,
They will decide what is good and bad,
They are the next prime minister, footballer and cleaner,
They will become adults,
Bright new ideas,
Instead of old,
A bright new world,
Instead of old,
No more wars,
No more racism,
No more gang wars,
No school uniform,
Healthy living,
Instead of junk food,
This is my generation, good as gold,
We are the world,
We are the future,
My generation.

Laurence Twell (12)
Neale Wade Community College, March

What It Is To Be British

I like fish and chips
I go to Brighton not Paris
We have football not soccer but the same
Nice trainers not sneakers
I use the motorway not the highway
I live my way.

My soul and life is British.

Anthony East (15)
Northfields Technology College, Dunstable

Full Of Sorrys Am I

I'm sorry I hit you and made you bleed
I'm sorry I made you cry
I was angry at that time I swear
I'm sorry that I lied.

All the things I have ever done
I wish I could take it back
I'm sorry that it's not my fault
For the physical problems I lack.

I look into the past and wonder about
How many times I hurt few
I'm sorry I damaged your soul so much
I didn't want that happening to you.

So I plead for your golden forgiveness
I'm begging for my last strife
I really hate to say this but
I'm sorry for living my life!

Shianele Abraham (13)
Northfields Technology College, Dunstable

Mole Hole

I got the ball and scored a goal,
As I was celebrating I tripped over a mole hole.
Everyone laughed, so did I,
But inside I wanted to cry.

I got the ball yet again,
Passed to the second top scorer Ben.
He had a shot, it hit the post,
It rebounded to me, I hit it towards the goal,
I scored, no I missed, so close, almost.

I got substituted, people cheered because I got a goal.
As I ran off I fell over the mole hole!

Rhys Stevens (13)
Northfields Technology College, Dunstable

Boys These Days

Bang, bang, in the head,
The flipping b*****ds must be dead,
Hit them, smack them with a bat,
Next thing you know they're all out flat.

They'll come back for a fight,
We will batter them all night,
We will chuck them in a pit
And make them eat all our s***.

Down goes another can,
Here comes another man,
He called us Tommy Tip,
That made us want to flip.

Oh no! Here come the cops,
They're approaching with armour tops,
Oh no! We have beer,
We become full of fear.

Run, run, run away,
I will drink beer another day,
Everyone hates police, they really do,
They don't even care about you.

Ryan Jefcoate (14)
Northfields Technology College, Dunstable

School

Sitting at school with my hands on my head,
Sitting there wishing I was still in my bed.
The teacher's at the front of the room,
I'm thinking about if the lesson will end soon.
I can't wait to get out to break
And sit with my mate Jake.
We all start to shout,
When we finally get out.

Kelly Ayliffe (14)
Northfields Technology College, Dunstable

When?

Sitting all alone,
As quiet as can be.
This old, empty home,
No one else, just me.

The siren goes off,
I panic and shout.
I sniff and cough,
I want to get out.

It breaks my heart,
Emotions scatter.
Houses fall apart,
What a terrible matter.

When will it stop?
When will it end?
When will our lives be on the mend?

Charlotte Cootes (13)
Northfields Technology College, Dunstable

I'm Sorry

I'm sorry I won't see you.
I like the way you are.
I'm sorry that I treated you this way.
I like the way you forgive me.
I'm sorry I hurt your feelings.
I like the way you keep secrets.
I'm sorry you're not here right now.
I like the way you know just how.

Stephen Cobb (15)
Northfields Technology College, Dunstable

War

Sitting in the corner,
I'm waiting for my life to restart.
I hear bombs go off
Also, the pounding of my heart.

I smell fear,
Rotting bodies too.
I can get through this
Lead it through.

I step outside,
Tried to miss a shot.
Damn! I missed
My soul he has now got!

Everything's a blur,
I can no longer see.
They pick me up,
There no longer is a 'me'!

Devon Kears (13)
Northfields Technology College, Dunstable

Untitled

In the sky the clouds will form
A dull and black windy storm
Down and down the rain will pour
Faster and faster and then even more
Soon the misery will turn into a smile
5 or 10 minutes, it's only a little while.

Jordan Back (13)
Northfields Technology College, Dunstable

I'm Sorry

I'm sorry for that day.
I'm sorry for when I ruined your play.
I'm sorry that I even turned up.
I'm sorry that you invited me.
I'm sorry for laughing at your acting.
I'm sorry I booed when you showed up on stage.
I'm sorry you felt ashamed and embarrassed.
I'm sorry for that day.

I'm sorry for that day.
I'm sorry I had a go.
I'm sorry I made your eye red
When we were playing in the snow.
I'm sorry I punched you.
I'm sorry I kicked.
I'm sorry you're bruised.
I'm sorry you're in hospital.
I'm sorry for that day.

I'm sorry for this poem.
I'm sorry it's so good.
I'm sorry you were attracted to it.
I'm sorry you didn't choose a different one.
I'm sorry for your choice of poem.
I'm sorry for you liking it.
I'm sorry this poem has to end.
I'm sorry for this poem.

I'm sorry it's the end.
I'm sorry, I'm sorry, I'm sorry.

Tom Wade (14)
Northfields Technology College, Dunstable

Teenage Life

Puff, puff, puff, puff,
Grind it up,
Bang it in,
Add the fag,
Lick the riz,
Roll it up,
Blaze away,
Wake up the next day.

Sip, sip, sip, sip,
Click the can,
Down the can,
Crush the can,
Throw the can,
Open up another can.

Bang, bang, bang, bang,
Up the stairs,
Lock the door,
Strip it down,
Bang it all around,
Make a lot of sound.

Spank, spank, spank, spank,
Here comes Mum,
Here comes Dad,
Out the door,
Slam the door,
I don't live there anymore.

Ben White (14)
Northfields Technology College, Dunstable

The Explosion On D-Day

The war was ending,
Hitler hung up his white flag,
But he still had one more card to play,
And it was to blow us away.

No one knew about this deadly sin,
Who would though?
He raised the detonator
And said to us on the Normandy banks,
'I'll see you later.'

Hitler then took his own life,
After making hundreds of women widows,
I stood there at the beach
Looking at the explosion on D-Day.

Ben Harper (13)
Northfields Technology College, Dunstable

Generation Gap

Back in my day
No PSP or Xbox
I always say
We made our amusements
We didn't have all these phones
We wrote a letter which is always better
Up at the crack of dawn
None of this out 'til four
Like I always say
Things were better
In my day.

Michael Johnston (15)
Northfields Technology College, Dunstable

War

Shrapnel flying,
Brave men dying,
Non-stop screams, orders and crying.

And here I am in the middle of it all,
Ordering men to move,
Trying to keep them from their last breath and fall.

Bullets fly past my face,
Taking my men, plants and trees,
Then suddenly I'm cold,
I fall to my knees,
And then I know my time has come,
My ticket out of this hell,
Straight from a gun,
I'm dead.

Jacob Kyte (13)
Northfields Technology College, Dunstable

I'm The Queen Of Me

I'm the Queen of Me,
I can do what I want,
Drink what I want, how much I want,
Do whatever I want,
Say what I want to whom I want,
Go wherever I want,
At what time I want, to see who I want,
Go out with the boy I want,
Don't care about what anyone else wants,
Because it's all about *what I want*.

Kayleigh Goodridge (14)
Northfields Technology College, Dunstable

War Poem

The moon rises high above a fearsome battle.
The bellowing sounds,
guns firing, bold soldiers yelling
and the sound of death fills the night
with an eerie symphony.
I overlook the scene and my eyes grow bold.
Smoke fills up the once fresh air
and the lifeless bodies are scattered all over the ground.
The foul taste of murky water splashes into my mouth,
as I run to rescue a fellow soldier.
I throw him over my shoulder and go to the nearest dugout.
As I enter, the room is filled with a disgusting odour,
the smell of excrement.
I lay the soldier on the bare ground.
No longer can I feel his heart pounding.
Blood all over my rough hands as I try to save him.
Why are they so cruel?

Megan McMahon (13)
Northfields Technology College, Dunstable

War Poem

Here I am, standing in the cold,
Rats scattering across the floor,
Hearing screams everywhere,
I feel dread and distraught all over,
Bang! Another life gone,
I feel so upset,
That person could have had family,
Children and friends,
Hundreds of people in agony.
The smell of rotten food,
The taste of fear,
All is horrible,
All is horrible.

Ellie Doherty (13)
Northfields Technology College, Dunstable

War Poem

Guns, trucks, planes,
People dying, people screaming,
The squelch of the cold mud,
The grey sky that lurks over the booming field,
It's alright, it's OK.

The person who stood next to me,
Communicating through his radio,
Saying . . . '09091 this is 09012,
Authorized to go in, 3, 2, 1.'

We raged onto the field,
Guns galore,
The booming field,
Was booming even more,
People were dying, people were screaming.

As I was running,
I stopped to say,
I will never forget this day.

10 years later,
We are stood here today,
We stop what we are doing,
And then we say,
We remember them!

Luke Holdstock (13)
Northfields Technology College, Dunstable

War

All those who've died
It hurts inside
While they die we live
Today all we give
A silence so brittle
Now I must say goodbye
And leave you with a question . . .
Why?

Taylor Wallace (13)
Northfields Technology College, Dunstable

Teenager Years

Teenager years are the best years of your life,
Apart from the people who go around with a knife,
Some are popular, and some are named a 'freak',
And there are those who religion they just 'seek'.
Everyone's unique, it's not hard to see,
That's why the world is what it is to me,
Teenagers, teenagers, why oh why,
Do you waste your life getting so high.
There's a whole world out there waiting for you,
So break free of the teenager years and always think things through.

Jayne Aris (14)
Northfields Technology College, Dunstable

The King Of The Football Field

I am the king, the king of the football field.
I have all the tricks and skills to make the crowd go wild.
My free kicks are amazing, my penalties are too.
Each throw in that I take is brilliantly placed,
Also, my corners are the best, they fly onto people's heads.
And yes, I am King of the football field.

Ashley Bloomfield (15)
Northfields Technology College, Dunstable

Sorry

I'm sorry I got up late
I'm sorry I was late for the bus
I'm sorry I was late for lesson
And I'm sorry I forgot my PE kit
I'm sorry I didn't hand in my homework
I'm sorry I got detention
I'm sorry I shouted at you like that
I'm sorry . . . I shouldn't have done any of that!

Nadine Sharp (15)
Northfields Technology College, Dunstable

War Is Never-Ending

War is never-ending
I leave myself with pain and heartbreak
Letting myself go through an unknown dark forest
Civil War trench echoes of the wind
Where they once threw 100 guns, waiting to kill me
I calm myself and fight for the country
As they kill me, a new war is just about to begin.

War is never-ending.

Kabelan Karunaseelan (13)
Northfields Technology College, Dunstable

Green Goblin Disgrace

Hate the green girl
Hate the way your ginger hair twirls
Hate the way you sneer
Hate the way your rear
Hangs out your skinny jeans
Hate the smell of your mouldy beans
Hate you just the way you are
Hate your green face
You are a goblin disgrace.

Kristen James (15)
Northfields Technology College, Dunstable

I'm Sorry And I Like . . .

I'm sorry I make you feel that way
I'm sorry for being so rude to you
I like to have you as a friend
I like the way you like to have a laugh
I'm sorry I ever doubted your thoughts
I'm sorry that I said you were dumb
I like coming to the party on your birthday
I like the way you take my breath away.

Andrew East (15)
Northfields Technology College, Dunstable

Devastation Of War

Perhaps you think you heard the story,
but no you haven't, it was far more gory.
The half-eaten story your grandpa told,
was burnt to ashes by fire so gold.
But never mind, his idea was right,
when bombs would fly and destroy the night.
The bodies that burned and houses that crumbled,
along with our loved ones would rumble and tumble.

But set aside the fires and deaths
and look at what we now have left.
Gone have our brothers, mothers and more,
this is the only devastation of war.

Penny Mitchell (14)
Northfields Technology College, Dunstable

Wartime

The splash of mud,
The taste of blood.
The grimy taste of iron,
All this just to save Private Ryan.

The weaponry you would have seen,
Who sends people to war? How mean.
The gritty sight of bodies scattered everywhere,
Just to conquer a bit of land, how unfair.

Just remember all the people who have died,
All the families who have cried.
So take some time to remember war,
Or get your grandads to tell you more.

Danniel Owen (13)
Northfields Technology College, Dunstable

Our Final Hour

Guns shoot
People dying
Husbands killed
Families crying.

The taste of blood is in the air
The slimy mud gets in my hair.

The sound of death
The smell of fear
I feel the end
The end is near.

The end is here
I feel the power
This here is our final hour.

Chris Dawkins (13)
Northfields Technology College, Dunstable

War City

The crashing waves
The army's slaves
That pour out from the city.

The dead men's graves
The army craves
The young men from the city.

The horse-like waves
The armies brave
That went back to the city.

Christopher Downes (13)
Northfields Technology College, Dunstable

The War

I lost my mother
I lost my father
I lost my sister
And lost my dreams too.

I touched my mother
I touched my father
I touched my sister
And I touched my last memories for the last time.

I could smell my mother's cooking
I could smell my father's smelly socks
I could smell my sister's perfume
And I am smelling my last remains of them.

I could hear my mother screaming
I could hear my father shouting
I could hear my sister crying
And I will never hear them again.

I could see my mother's necklace
I could see my father's ring
I could see my sister's teddy
And I will never see them again.

I lost my mother
I lost my father
I lost my sister
And now they will lose me.

I will pray for them all the time
But now is the time to go
Send on our wishes
Off to the grave I go.

Adam Ilsley (13)
Northfields Technology College, Dunstable

War Poem

I can see the fear in the enemy,
I can hear the cries for life,
I can taste the stench of smoke,
I can feel the itchy, dried mud stuck to my face.

I can hear the scream from the shells above,
I can taste the sweat rolling down my cheeks,
I miss my family so much, I just want to scream,
I smell the reek of the rotting dead,
I see no end to this madness.

Tom Allmett (13)
Northfields Technology College, Dunstable

My Trench

I have a little wet home, a trench
Where the rain continuously falls
With just mud for a bed
With no warmth or shelter.

They know we're here to stay
They shoot and they shout
But they can't get us out
Though there is no game we can't play.

Yes we think of the cold, slush and stench
As we play with the Belgians and French
But there be shed of fear
Much worse than a tear
My little wet home, the trench.

Guy Rayment (13)
Northfields Technology College, Dunstable

My Generation

Generations like mine seem different than they were a long time ago,
we didn't have to deal with war or food rations or being evacuated.
It was just smooth sailing for most of us.

As children we would cook pretend meals for families,
bounce up and down until we went green on our bounce hoppers.
As we got older we would ride bikes,
go on holidays and go to theme parks.
It seemed just a smooth and effortless life,
but sometimes happy families got broken.

Kids these days don't ride their bikes down their streets
or play with their friends as much as they used to.
They are usually glued in front of the TV, PlayStation,
computer and other video games, often alone.
I however go outside and ride my bike and play with my friends,
I am lucky to live in a safe neighbourhood,
with little traffic to worry about.
Also nowadays you have to be careful
about strange people walking about,
but I feel safe where I live because everybody knows each other.

Family values are changing.
Nowadays a lot of the population of young people
have come from broken families.
Some mothers are forced to go to work to provide food,
water and shelter for their children.
Others because they want a career and to be successful.
Also in our society today we are encouraged to want more
than we have already.
With lots of help from advertisements.

Children in this generation seem unhappy with who they are
and want to grow up faster.
Drinking, drugs and underaged pregnancies
are a very worrying problem that can play a big part
in young people's lives today.
I'm not going to let that effect mine.

I want to enjoy being young and playing with my friends
and to remember the things that are important in life.

Although society can affect our lives,
I am grateful to come from a family
that still cherishes the togetherness of family.

Eloise Austin (12)
Peterborough High School, Peterborough

Talkin' 'Bout My Generation

Well what can I say about my generation?

You can't play in the park
Let alone in the wood
Leave the house, with no mobile
As if we could?

You can't look at a stranger
For fear of a knife
Imagine being worried
For the rest of your life.

The youth of today
Wear trackies and caps
They have nothing to say
But 'ight mate? and *Brap!*

You've got hairspray and make-up
They think they look cool
Speak back to the teachers
And skive whole days off school.

Sidney Thomas (12)
Peterborough High School, Peterborough

Talkin' 'Bout My Generation

Talking about my generation can be either of two things,
It can be sad and depressing or it can be fun with what it brings.
My poem is going to be about both sides of the story,
About it now and what it was like in its former glory.

Nowadays a lot of things are dark and scary,
There are plenty of situations where you have to be wary,
But back in the day everything was fine,
You'd wake up in the morning and the sun would shine.

The day to day crime in today's population,
Is more than enough to fill prisons, let alone police stations,
Back in the day worst you would get is a couple of house burglaries,
Not murderers and terrorists from overseas.

We turn on the news and hear such and such is dead;
There was a shooting on his street, he got three bullets
                                        through his head.
Back in the day it was an enormous tragedy,
The whole nation would mourn all in unity.

In today's society a lot has been said,
About how what we are doing to the world is making it dead,
The autopsy reads global warming and pollution,
But back in the day there was no need for a solution.

Now don't get me wrong I'm not saying my generation is all bad,
There are plenty of things our parents never had,
Back in the day they didn't have PlayStations
                                and Game Boys galore,
They had to work their way out of a bore.

And let's face it, today we're lucky with information,
We get it easy and as for communication,
Back in the day mobiles were distant;
Now for us kids they're so so persistent.

But before I go I must tell you;
This isn't the whole story of my generation.
It's just 33 lines of its real sensation!

Megan Chittock (13)
Peterborough High School, Peterborough

Talking About My Generation

The world is quite a scary place for a 12-year-old girl,
With people bombing places like London and Glasgow,
Peace has just flown out the window.

By the age of 14 you are thinking about what you want to do
                                                    when you're older,
In the old days it did not matter,
It's barely safe to play out on the streets anymore,
With children older and younger than us going missing.

Nowadays we go abroad so often,
But back then the furthest you went from your home in England,
Was Scotland, but now we go to places like Australia?

Back then you could climb a tree,
And scrape your knee,
But nobody would care.

If you fell and broke your arm
It would heal by itself.
If you break your arm now,
It's straight to A&E!

The world today isn't safe,
With wars going on everywhere,
Family or friends in the RAF, Navy or Army off to Iraq,
To fight the wars that other people start.

Schools aren't the same anymore,
You hang out with certain people,
And don't have a chance to meet other people,
So when you all fall out you don't have anyone else to talk to.

We think that everyone is so different,
But actually they're not, we play and talk,
Even though we sound different,
Or talk with different tongues,
We are all the same deep down inside.

Megan Orme-Smith (13)
Peterborough High School, Peterborough

The Grandma Vs Children Debate

'It wasn't like that when I was young.
We'd be up by the crack of dawn.
I wouldn't have done that,' they moan.
'They're not the clothes I would have worn.'
The children think a little about their rebuttal,
'Well, maybe we're not perfect,
But we mind our ps and qs.
What would you have worn then?'
Grandmas jumping to their feet!
'We'd have worn proper practical shoes.'
'But what about Nike?'
A plucky, quiet yet scary kid jumps up from the back,
Slowly pushed down by the glare of a scarier Grandma.
'Nike . . . no such thing!'
'Our mothers' made our clothes.'
'And what about ya' bling?'
Nike kid is on his feet yet again!
'At least we have fun these days!
Like you say, you were up at the crack of dawn.
You were all proper and practical,
We don't care what you would have worn!
If you didn't have Nike you must all have looked like mingers!'
'Gerald! Really, a little respect please.
Class dismissed, in next week's debate class
The topic is 'Homework; pros and cons'. Come prepared.'

Grace Sandys (13)
Peterborough High School, Peterborough

My Generation Poem

My generation,
Our generation,
We are all so lucky,
We all get to go to school,
Or get a good job,

Our stomach's always full,
Our throat's never dry,
Our parents normally have a car,
Maybe two or even three,
Most families have their own pet,

Are we all too lucky?

Will we be even luckier in the future?
Instead of driving a normal car we could all have limousines,
Or when our parents take us to school we could
                              be taken by bodyguards!
But back to my generation.

Gangsters graffiti every wall they can see,
Pets being abandoned,
Litter everywhere we step,
We e-mail instead of sending letters,

Are we abusing our luck?
Are we abusing my generation?
Are we abusing our generation?

Lucy Blatchford (12)
Peterborough High School, Peterborough

What Has Happened To The World?

What has happened to the world?
Why do we get dragged in,
By this evil world,
Which smoking and drugs are in?

What has happened to the world?
Why are we so scared,
To walk the streets alone
With people in hoodies out there?

What has happened to the world?
Destroyed by graffiti,
'What are we meant to do?' they say
Well play with you and me.

What has happened to the world?
Is it really better?
Have children improved on their behaviour?
What has happened to the world?

Florentyne Barrett (13)
Peterborough High School, Peterborough

Generations

They think of us as hoodies,
Who just drink and smoke,
They think we shout and swear,
To them it's some kind of joke!

They went out late with their friends,
We have to stay inside,
They wore dungarees - the latest trend,
We wear our jeans with pride.

We think they're rather lucky,
They were happy and carefree,
We're the ones stuck with the rules,
Think how hard that must be!

Anoushka Edirisooriya (13)
Peterborough High School, Peterborough

Talking About My Generation

PlayStations, Motorolas, Nintendos and TV,
All big things in the lives of you and me.

Chavs, emos and goths too,
Which one of them are you?

Chilling and relaxing all alone,
Sometimes left by myself, here at home.

Summer holidays hanging with friends,
School starts, fun ends.

Football, hockey and netball as well,
Without these school would be hell.

Technology, maths and IT,
Two years later, GCSE.

School trips,
Rainy, wet dips.

Graffiti, vandalism,
Cheating, plagiarism.
All these acts are wrong,
This is the generation where I belong.

Pooja Seta (12)
Peterborough High School, Peterborough

Generations To Come

Space walkers,
Flying cars,
Astronauts in the stars,

Future, future, Jupiter and Mars

Space stations
And teleportation,
Robotic automation,

Future, future, this is all in our imagination.

Holly Lawler (11)
Peterborough High School, Peterborough

The Different Generations

The world has changed since our mothers were kids
No more go-karts made from dustbin lids
A lot of technology, apologies and crime
No more lead water pipes - what a waste of time!

My grandad set off fireworks when he was little
He played lots of sports, like football and skittles
He'd never seen an iPod, DVD or Sky
He acted in plays and tried to fly

My father climbed trees and played lots of games
He played for a team and they dreamt of fame
He got told off by parents, teachers and staff
He was the type of person that wanted a laugh

My family doesn't change as you move through the generations
Even though we all live in different directions
We all like to joke, mess about and play
We are all the same at the end of the day.

Bethany Cameron (12)
Peterborough High School, Peterborough

50 Years Ago And Now

Kids in fields and down the lane,
Playing with friends in the sunshine or rain,
Home-made race carts,
Playing near the lake,
Playing climbing trees
And filling up on sweets and cake.
Going round a friend's house
Without telling Mum,
Playing out all day,
But back before the street lamps come on.

Back from school and homework done,
18 hours of TV a week,
Really isn't that much fun.
Mobile phones and MSN,
Your friends text to you and you email them.
Rebellious teens and
ASBOs for hanging around,
T-shirts and jeans,
Those iPods make a noisy sound.
But really, even when they drive you mad,
The technology literate generation really isn't all that bad.

Gemma Rate (13)
Peterborough High School, Peterborough

My Generations

Years ago,
People used their feet to get around
But it wasn't long before the horse and cart was found
Children played with sticks all day
With nothing much to eat.

Now, in the present tense,
Cars get us from A to B
It's electronic games we play
Supermarkets everywhere, so lots of food to eat.

Things have changed through the generations
Will this ever stop?
Who knows what will happen in the future
What changes are to be made?
What will my children see?

Katie Ivens (11)
Peterborough High School, Peterborough

Talkin' 'Bout My Generation

'I'm bored!'
We shout
But we're not allowed out
We might be kidnapped or attacked
Is that so?

Some people just want to have fun
Others are just a bore
'Hoodies and bullies should be locked up in jail,'
Says Granny!
They used to be free to do what they liked
Our parents are too overprotective.

We can't go out and stay out for hours.
But they could!

You did so why can't I?

Chloe King (13)
Peterborough High School, Peterborough

Trapped

Love, a funny thing,
It never changes,
But the situation does,
The world changes around love,
Making people paranoid and scared,
Parents, not letting us out,
Because of the people out there,
In case you get hurt in any way,
Fall off your bike, graze your knee,
Oh how awful that would be!
The dangers of the world made them stronger,
How will deprivation of those dangers affect us?
Will it make us weak in life?

I want to get out!
Get out of this safe zone,
Have more risk in life,
Climb a mountain, go sky diving,
Live life to the full,
Playing safe *and* living dangerously,
Help! I'm trapped!
Trapped in a cage of protective love.

Molly Adam (13)
Peterborough High School, Peterborough

Generation Poem

G enerations have changed so much;
E lectronics at a touch.
N ow we have PlayStations and mp3s too -
E verything but lovely fresh air will do.
R unning around getting mud on our hands,
A few children noisier than three brass bands.
T oday, we have mobiles - small, not thick -
I n the old days they were like a house brick.
O ld cars spacious, lots of room
N ew cars have the 'va va voom'.

Micheala Drazek (12)
Peterborough High School, Peterborough

Talkin' 'Bout My Generation

'Come this way child!
I will tell you 'bout my generation!
25 years ago . . .'
Back in those days, we were free as a bird;
We caught innocent frogs and dragonflies.
We screamed and yelled but nobody heard,
We played wildly without catching one's eyes . . .
That was the beauty of *my* generation!

We met in our usual hide-out spot,
Nearby our small friendly mate: the lake,
In the dark and silent night with the stunning moonshine,
We leapt, naked, into the welcoming water,
Oh, how *wonderful* it was then!

Generations, to generations . . . it seems like a lifetime!
'Lifetime' is long enough to change ways of living
'Ways of living' began from freedom
'Freedom' was *my* generation . . .

Then this 'child'; a little 'un from the *modern* generation,
Says to me sweetly and confidently,
'It sounds all *fun*, and *cool*, and great, yes it does,
But you see, I like *my* generation!
Shopping, watching movies, doing makeovers . . .
Coolness is all that matters to me!
Meeting friends outside and being late coming back home . . .
Funny, how my parents fuss over me though!
All I need to make me feel safe is . . .
Just my *'fully-charged mobile phone!'*

Ji Young Hwang (13)
Peterborough High School, Peterborough

About My Generation

In my generation we can't go out
without a talk from Mum,
or stay out to play with friends
until the streetlamps come on.
Apparently we steal from shops
and wear hoodies all the time,
we answer back to teachers
and we swear from time to time.

In my generation we can't eat
sweets with too much sugar in,
we can't go out to play in the snow
because of health and safety.
Apparently we smoke, drink
and have multiple body piercings,
also we take illegal drugs
and go around breaking things.

But I don't see how mums and dads
get all these silly stories,
because actually we're much better
than when they were kids in the sixties.
When they were kids they were allowed
to do whatever they wanted,
but I don't see how it is fair
if we can't do what they did.

Hannah Diver (13)
Peterborough High School, Peterborough

A Generation Poem

Sweets, fizzy drinks and fast food,
Are lovely once in a while,
Sadly too much is eaten and gets me down,
And the obesity rate has run a mile.

Crime rate high,
Respect rate low,
Wars make people sigh,
And everyone has more than one foe.

Nintendos and Xboxes cheer us up,
Better education at school,
New hairstyles and clothes make it worth waking up,
And McDonald's make us drool.

TVs, DVDs and video games,
Cinema and the theatre show,
More benefit claims,
Swimming pools to the garden hose.

Lucille Kenny (12)
Peterborough High School, Peterborough

My Generation Sensation

G reat toys or so they thought
E ating pocket money sweets
N o real laws except for school
E xciting adventures, danger everywhere
R unning and playing, broken bones
A nd thrill and canes
T rick and treat? Smell my feet
I n case you're wondering
O f whose generation I'm on about
N o longer is it here, it's now only memories and maybe tears

S o now on to my generation
E ating junk food and burping robotic babies
N o more real fun but law's changed that
S o who recycles? I do
A nd the rest of us? Not all
T hey made all the mess, why should we clean it up?
I n time we will see
O h how bad we have all been
N o I don't like my generation, but for one thing, it's safer.

Ellie Raby-Smith (12)
Peterborough High School, Peterborough

My Generation

The children playing inside and out
With lots of shouting and screaming about
With new gadgets and fun things to do
The mothers and fathers telling you to move
Bikes and skateboards lying about
With new discoveries yet to be found

Children eating three meals a day
Mothers calling children Fay and May
Education, work and school
Whilst sitting on fancy stools
Clocks ticking now and then
Little kids buying Barbie and Ken

Clothes, dresses, headbands and tops
Nothing to do with cold wet mops
Mum washing dishes, knives and forks
Dad pulling out the wine cork
Food and water
Mum getting short
This life is worth living.

Victoria Thorpe Jones (12)
Peterborough High School, Peterborough

My Generation

We wear hoodies
and eat goodies.
We stay out late
and go on dates.

We see films
and go out shopping,
while we paint our nails
in colours most shocking.

A passion for fashion,
a passion for fashion.
Why oh why
do we have such a passion for fashion?

We love . . .
styling our hair
while we sit in a beautician's chair.

We want everything to be fabulous.

Zara Tosh (13)
Peterborough High School, Peterborough

My Generation

'Fancy a cup of tea?' Auntie May asked.
'No thanks Auntie, I'm off to Flo's house;
Must go straight away!
I'll party all night, right through twilight. If that's okay?
But I probably shouldn't ask you - cos I'll go anyway,
No matter what you say!
And don't expect me back for many a day.'

'Want to play snooker?' Grandad Benny asked.
'No offence Gramps, but snooker's not that good a game.
Why not try my Xbox?
Or have a pile of fun, just dancing in the rain?
You could have a go on 'Sims' - it's my favourite computer game
But you probably wouldn't like it; you're far too lame
. . . And let's face it - you're not exactly sane!'

'Want a round of golf Beth? It's the perfect time of day!'
'Really sorry Dad, but I'm afraid I cannot lie. (I think I'd rather die.)
But now I feel so guilty - you're really such a nice guy.
I think I'll just listen to some music.
(Before I start to lose it.)
Britney, Whitney, Rhianna and Timbaland.
Why not lend a hand. Come on Dad! What's your favourite band?'

'You're poorly! Don't eat cake! It would be a serious mistake!'
'Don't worry Mum - only one I'll take.
They're so nicely baked . . .
They must help my cough . . .
They're so lovely and soft.
Who could resist them - emos, chavs or goths?
Please Mum, there is nothing better than chocolate
Around my chops!'

Bethany Johnson (13)
Peterborough High School, Peterborough

My Generation

Technology has come far,
With many different types of car.
There's so many Nintendos, there's PlayStation and Wii,
Let alone the improvements in ICT.

So what else does my generation bring?
I bet all of you would think of a different thing.
Some of improvements, some of happiness,
Others of yobs, crime and distress.

Now if you wear a hoodie,
And you are out at night,
You must be about to commit an offence,
Surely this isn't right.

For some, unfortunately it's true,
But for others not at all.
They may just want to look like their friends,
Or fit in or be cool.

So next time you pass a hoodie,
You may want to run and hide,
But think about the person,
What's there? What's inside?

There are good and bad parts to my generation,
Such as considerable developments in many things,
But also an increase in crime and unrest,
So I don't think my generation is the worst but not the best.

Sophie Wilson (12)
Peterborough High School, Peterborough

Generations

My mum's generation
Out to play 'til five.
My generation
Cooped up inside.

My mum's generation
Snowball fights galore.
My generation
Obsessed with the safety law.

My mum's generation
No seatbelts in the car.
My generation
Belted up no matter how far.

My mum's generation
Fawn cords - Mum's favourite pair.
My generation
Jeans with bolt straight hair.

My mum's generation
Happy and carefree.
My generation
Are we?

Emily Yong (14)
Peterborough High School, Peterborough

Generations Of Music

They listened to The Beatles,
We listen to McFly,
They listened to The Police
And we listen to Fall Out Boy.

They listened to Nirvana,
We listen to Blink 182,
They listened to Smashing Pumpkins
And we listen to My Chemical Romance.

They listened to Spice Girls,
We listen to Girls Aloud,
They listened to Charlotte Church
And we listen to Hannah Montana.

They listened to Queen,
We listen to Mika,
They listened to David Bowie
And we listen to Panic! At The Disco.

The generations might change,
The bands might change,
The music might change,
But the notes stay the same.

Aarti Patel (13)
Peterborough High School, Peterborough

Mind The Generation Gap

What does 'age' think of 'youth'?
'They're hooded yobs,
And drunken slobs.
Knife using,
Drug abusing,
The ASBO generation.'

What does 'age' think of 'age'?
'We're kind and mature,
Hardworking, demure.
Completely sensible,
Indispensable,
The useful generation.'

What does 'youth' think of 'age'?
'They're old and they're stodgy,
Controlling and bossy.
Over-protective,
Under-effective,
The hypocrite generation.'

What does 'youth' think of 'youth'?
'We're falsely accused,
Our image abused.
Media controlled,
Police patrolled,
The misunderstood generation.'

Susannah Lewis (14)
Peterborough High School, Peterborough

Reminiscing

Flying down the hill at 20 miles an hour
Knowing that at the bottom
The turnout may be dire
But just for the excitement
And just for going fast
You speed down the hill
On your rusty
Home-made
Go-kart.

You say goodbye to Mummy
And say farewell to Dad
Why do you let your children out?
The neighbours think you're mad.

Walking down the street one night
Wishing you weren't alone
You spot a gang of hoodies
Drinking by the road
You cross the road to miss them
But they see you all the same
They shout and swear and throw things.
It's 'kill the victim' game.

I sprint past the churchyard
My heartbeat in my ears
A quick look behind me
And he's still closely near
I run past the duck pond
And struggle up the hill
At the top I give up
And sit in the dark on my bill
I hold up my white flag . . .
Tag!

Ellie Wood (13)
Peterborough High School, Peterborough

Generation Poem

Dunnaa dunnaa do dunna,
There's a disco rolling in the air,
Do dunnaa do dunna,
Everyone's got their hands punching the sky.

Bunnaa bunnaa bo bunnaa,
Look at the dancer's wacky hair-do,
Bo bunnaa bo bunnaa,
Fashion sense was everything in this time.

Punnaa punnaa po punnaa,
The goths are in the corner over there,
Po punnaa po punnaa,
All in black doing ghostly moves.

Funnaa funnaa fo funnaa,
The girls screech and woo! for the teddy boys,
Fo funnaa fo funnaa,
Who was having fun showing off their hair?

These were my dad's prime years,
He liked to dance around with his chums,
It was like this in the 1970s,
Now it's approaching 4am, *shhh sha sha shhh shhh.*

Tabitha McNulty-Skead (11)
Peterborough High School, Peterborough

Generation

Smiles, laughter and fun
All these words may mean nothing,
But if you stop and think,
Realise what they mean,
Everyone in a stage of their life would have come across it,
If you go back in the sixties,
Parents wouldn't have to worry,
Wouldn't have to worry about their children,
On the news today,
We'd hear the words *kidnapped, bombings, rape,*
This is such a worry to parents now,
Children can't just go outside and go around the block,
They would have to be supervised,
Many of us don't actually know what is going on anymore,
Some people waste their time taking drugs and alcohol,
What a way to end your life, when it has only just begun.
As life goes on,
Our generation is constantly changing
And it will never be the same.

Becky Dennis (14)
Peterborough High School, Peterborough

Talkin' 'Bout The Dance Generation

Hipin', hoppin', jivin', slidin',
Body poppin', rhythm ridin'.

Shoo ob a bob, ring a ding de dong,
The 'hand jive' generation,
Twistin' low 'n' long,
The 50s dances of the nation.

Hipin', hoppin', jivin', slidin',
Body poppin', rhythm ridin'.

Do doobie do, a rockin' 'n' rollin',
The 'locomotion' that has lasted many generations,
The 60s hippies strollin',
When dance had reputations.

Hipin', hoppin', jivin', slidin',
Body poppin', rhythm ridin'.

Rock, rock, punkin' on down,
The dance rebels' generation,
Funkin' up the beat, makin' elders frown,
The 70s children rockin' the nation.

Hipin', hoppin', jivin', slidin',
Body poppin', rhythm ridin'.

Dance fever boogieing' 'round,
Joinin' the 'Wham' generation,
'The Time Warp' was found,
The 80s disco plagued the nation.

Hipin', hoppin', jivin', slidin',
Body poppin', rhythm ridin'.

Shoo ob, do, rockin' 'n' dancin' about,
Talkin' 'bout the dance generation,
Ten centuries, one millennium,
The dances of the past, present and future
Parade through the nation.

Hipin', hoppin', jivin', slidin',
Body poppin', rhythm ridin'.

Enjoyment is what it's all about!

Chloë Laycock (11)
Peterborough High School, Peterborough

My Generation Should I Say?

Well in my generation there's not much to say
We're all angels in the day
Oh and we adore having to play
We sit outside admiring the birds
Looking out for all the sheep in herds
That's all really, nothing else to say
Unless you want to know more,
Should I say?

Well the side you know isn't so great
It's the one most of you hate
The one that's over the media
Type it into Wikipedia if you want more
But anyway, the side that I said before we all hate
Is the one with the teenagers and such
But millions of *my* generation aren't like that
But how do I know?
Do they put it on for a show?

Simran Kaur Nanuwa (11)
Peterborough High School, Peterborough

Talkin' 'Bout My Generation

Talkin' 'bout my generation
in the library, people look
hard for a book, book.

Talkin' 'bout my generation
when I shout and scream
asking Mum and Dad for ice cream, ice cream.

Talkin' 'bout my generation
astronauts go to the moon
will they come back soon, soon?

Talkin' 'bout my generation
having beans in a pod
with battered cod.

Talkin' 'bout my generation
cheetahs are going too fast
in such a long past, past.

Talkin' 'bout my generation
builders wanting to bore me
asking more, more.

Talkin' 'bout my generation
I want to dance 'n' sing
in da season of spring, spring.

Pavna Venugopal (11)
Peterborough High School, Peterborough

My Generation

T he generation today is unlike any generation gone before it.
O utside play has gone away, now we're stuck indoors to stay.
D Ss, Xboxes and iPods, we love them all.
   Technology's making the world fall
A nti-aging products, anti-wrinkle creams being made
   to sort our insecurities.
Y ouths hanging around with nothing else to do,
   waiting for their opportunity to brew.

A nti-social behaviour causing the community
   to have a bad flavour
N ature reserves and conservation issues
   making your heart melt and grabbing some tissues
D estruction and disrespect all making us think and reflect

N HS services which are here to help,
   doctors that can make you yelp
O verall the world today is a lot better than the world yesterday
W e are the present and the future, the leaders,
   the health professionals, the people that will and can help.

Katie Jeffs (13)
Peterborough High School, Peterborough

My Generation

My generation
My generation are a funny lot,
We yell, we scream, we shout so loud that the neighbours complain,
We turn our music up to full volume in the dead of night,
And we love to lark about,
That's my generation.

My generation
My generation are a funny lot,
We talk like dis and tht,
We have no manners,
We are always wantin' more,
That's my generation.

The middle generation,
The middle generation scare us,
They scare us so we don't want to go out,
They make our parents worry about our safety,
That's the middle generation.

The middle generation,
The middle generation swear
And take over the parks,
Use them as dens where they lie in wait like a dragon in its lair,
That's the middle generation.

My parents' generation,
My parents' generation used to run around in the street
For the middle generation for them was not quite so fierce,
They too loved to scream and shout,
So loud that their joyful cries pierced the air,
That's my parents' generation.

And now you can see that we're not so different after all.

Bethan Youens (12)
Peterborough High School, Peterborough

Becoming A Teen

Becoming a teen,
Means you are seen,
Whenever or wherever you go.
If you're wearing a hoodie people judge,
When all you want to do is buy some fudge.
You feel everyone's your foe.

In the 50s and 60s becoming a teen,
Means you could go back wherever you'd been.
Nowadays though it's not the same.
You go outside, it starts to rain,
You really start to feel the pain.
Back then, though, if it rained, you could make it a big game.

Today you'd see a teenager,
Typing something in on their pager,
Because technology's growing.
Back then they'd all got
A piece or two of the plot,
Because the wind isn't blowing.

So if you see a teen today,
Just smile, wave and say 'hey',
But in a friendly way.
So if you see a teen in a shop,
Don't smile and say 'I've got to hop',
Just let them browse, it's OK.

Sheringham Reynolds (12)
Peterborough High School, Peterborough

Talkin' 'Bout My Generation

Generations, let's talk about,
Yours and mine,
Let's scream and shout,
About the huge long line,

Ma generation, talks like dis,
Wat up chump? Let's fling some disc
Some can't keep a convo up,
Wat's wrong wif dese ppl - wat's up chump?

My nanna used to tell me so,
Of her generation - that one you know,
So let's see how they used to speak,
Maybe it won't give you the creep!

They used to talk all sssspick and sssspan,
She told me they had to, but oh how they can,
Their Ss were all long and clean,
Sounding like snakesss through all what time has been.

Me and her were very close,
Both of us we loved the most,
But couldn't speak to her when I tried
I lost her forever,
In the jungle of time . . .

Generations, let's talk about,
Yours and mine,
I lost hers but you can find mine,

Now you know my story,
Tell the lil ones too,
Of how we struggle to communicate,
All under one big roof.

Sehar Nazir (11)
Peterborough High School, Peterborough

Talkin' 'Bout My Generation!

Generation after generation
This never stops
A beginning to a new generation
This is a generation attained by me.

Crying, screaming tears from my eyes
I'm born, this is a surprise
Looking at the people around me
Wow! Giants they are, that's what I can see.

Skyscrapers
Fast, speeding cars
Flying papers
Children on bars.

'Dis is cool,' da man says
As he lays
Dis is how dey talk
Wid a slight angle of a walk.

The generation is about fashion as it glows
This is how it is, this is how it flows
Fast food around us 24/7
The gorgeous McFlurry made in Heaven.

McBurgers, McFries
Mc everything you don't need to sigh
Big Macs 'n' drinks, take some sips
Just eat it all and remember to lick your lips.

So that's it, I'm growing big but not too tall
I'm creeping in to catch the generation ball
This is it, I have to bow
This is how I live now!

Marya Yousaf (11)
Peterborough High School, Peterborough

My Generation

Lucky, yeah right!
Wish we could play outside day and night.
It is not as safe anymore,
Parents worry as soon as we shut the door.

In the 40s fun came cheap,
Over the fields we'd run and leap.
Nowadays fun is expensive,
The list of gadgets required is extensive.

Skipping, leapfrog, hide-and-seek,
That would keep the oldies happy for a week!
We have PlayStations, iPods and a television,
After 24 hours we are so bored we'd rather do revision!

As you can see life has got complicated,
I think the gadgets of the 21st century are overrated.
Life in the old days sounds a blast,
I wish I could click my fingers and be in the past.

Hollie Ismail (12)
Peterborough High School, Peterborough

My Generation

My generation is old,
My generation is new,
My generation is all things old and new.

From Xbox 360s,
To toys that can fly,
That's nothing compared to my iPod and Sky.

From high street fashion,
To charity shops,
Buying clothes is the tops.

Hanging out on street corners,
Or playing in the garden,
I've still got good manners and always say 'pardon'.

Spots and braces are a pain;
Doesn't matter unless you're vain,
Just keep smiling in the rain.

Being a teenager can be tough,
But this doesn't mean you have to be rough!

Ruth Plant (13)
Peterborough High School, Peterborough

My Generation

Generation, generation, this is my generation,
The generation of technology and computers,
The generation of hovercrafts and voice-controlled cars,
The time of mind wave-controlled computers and changeable
                                              pens to pencils.

Generation, generation, this is my generation,
The generation of microchip CDs and the only cars are limos,
The generation of a healthy Earth where acid rain falls rarely
                                              and smoking is band.

Generation, generation, this is my generation,
The generation of motorbikes with safety rules and pubs
                                              with licences,
The generation of free TV and solar powered houses.

Generation, generation, this is my generation,
The generation of good times and bad times but definitely not war,
A generation where the ozone layer is slowly rebuilding
                                              and the people getting on.

This is the generation I would like to live in . . .
My generation!

Emma Heys (11)
Peterborough High School, Peterborough

Talkin' 'Bout My Generation

The world is so different today,
There are many more people,
There are lots of things to explore,
I don't know what to say.

Cars zooming all around,
Electricity running through houses,
TVs, radios, Game Boys,
All making a very loud sound.

People used to be entertained
By nature and books,
It was all very quiet,
The world was not polluted like today
And now there are so many crooks.

The world is so different today,
There are many more people,
I wonder if it will change again,
Or if it will stay this way?

Ellie-Rose Fowler (11)
Peterborough High School, Peterborough

Talking 'Bout My Generation

Father, Mother, Sister, Brother,
Family, friends, one or the other.
Dog, cat, fish, rabbit,
Talking like this is my old habit.

Grandpa, Grandma, Uncle, Aunt,
Stop talking like this! 'No,' I shout.
Cousins, niece, nephews too,
Talking like this is the way I do.

Son, Brother, Daughter-in-Law,
Dogs howling, holding up their paw.
Sitting down with photo albums,
Thinking 'bout your generation.

Talking 'bout my generation,
Feeding you with information,
When the skies are blue like this,
This old lecture, you cannot miss!

Sreejoyee Roychowdhury (11)
Peterborough High School, Peterborough

Our Generation, Their Generation

The 21st century can be a bore.
All the channels, the movies and PlayStation games.
Nobody outside, playing games.
The last generation is different by far.

Our mums and dads would go out for hours,
No one could reach them all day.
Now there are warnings, kidnappers and more,
Who changed this generation?

Our generation, their generation,
Separated by technology and laws.
Our generation, their generation,
Where did it all go wrong?

Imogen Hallett (12)
Peterborough High School, Peterborough

Like Our Parents' Generation

Some people say we're all bad,
Not enough respect,
Labelled with ASBOs,
Why can't we be like them?

Too obsessed with Bebo, YouTube;
Not enough fresh air,
Where's the exercise?
Why can't we be like them?

Get too much technology,
Loads of MSN,
Hundreds of iPods,
Why can't we be like them?

Alas, we can still have fun!
We know how to climb trees,
We can build our dens!
Who wants to be like them?

Serena Ward (12)
Peterborough High School, Peterborough

Our Generation

In the 50s, 60s and 70s,
There were no high-tech computers,
Just a black and white TV,
With only four channels,
To keep them company all day.

There's no playing out after 6pm
In case we get attacked or kidnapped,
There's no playing in the roads,
Without getting battered and bruised.

We have fancy food packets,
You just put them in the microwave,
And they only take a few minutes!

Natasha van Uden (13)
Peterborough High School, Peterborough

The Generation Difference

'Do you know where my computer is Mum?'
'Haven't you two got something better to do?'
'Well we could listen to my iPod,
But we'd run out of songs to listen to, bored in a few.
Please Mum, what else could we do?'

'Well when I was your age, I'd go biking,
And how I loved roller skating down the street!
The field opposite Gran's was my favourite place though,
We played rounders, tag, stuck in the mud and all.
Shame we don't have a field round here, you know.'

'Agreed Mum, can we go biking then?
That sounds really fun! Where should we go Molly?
We could ride down the muddy run!
Or ride round the church and stop at the village green!
Oh let's go to Amelia's and see how she's been!'

'Not without me you're not, it's dangerous out there!
You could be run over, those cars on that busy road,
Or you could be abducted; now there's a horrid thought!
If you go riding too fast, you'll fall off your bike.
The sight of grazed knees is not something I like.'

'Why can't we go Mum?
Why would we not be careful on the road?
Or stopping to chat to someone we don't know?
And you have seen us ride our bikes before!
Do you not realise Mum, you're such a bore!

'Things have changed now and I'm over protective,
Things could happen and I'm not there to help.
But playing on the PlayStation is not nearly as much fun,
As playing with your friends in the evening sun!
And as long as you are careful, go out and have some fun!'

Katie Parkin (12)
Peterborough High School, Peterborough

My Generation

My generation is all about what you wear.
If it's not about clothes, it's how you do your hair.
There are designer, high street or supermarket brands.
I wish we could just run around, get mud on our hands.

Xbox 360, PlayStation 3.
Game Boys, videos, Nintendo Wii.
We should go out more, play on our bikes,
Making the most of the light summer nights.

Picture phones, iPods, egg chairs galore.
Money is everything, no hand-me-downs anymore.
No dens, no bruises, no football on the street.
Those were the days when we could get dirty feet.

My generation is all about what you wear.
If it's not about clothes, it's how you do your hair.
There are designer, high street or supermarket brands.
I wish we could just run around, get mud on our hands.

Becci Jeffers (12)
Peterborough High School, Peterborough

My Generation

G reat buildings and gadgets,
E ndangering wildlife and animals,
N ever saying sorry for what we've done.
E nough of pollution and killing,
R ushing for what we want, never thinking.
A n atlas of the ever-changing world;
T ime is speeding along.
I n my life I have seen so many wonderful things,
O n my own, I now know I will never,
N ever leave this world without being proud!

Charlotte Shoemake (12)
Peterborough High School, Peterborough

War Is Human

War is human and human is war,
Our race's inescapable, unwritten law.

Battle resounds from every level,
From the soldier's deep voice to the infant's shrill treble.

Name him as you please, War is a must,
He makes Man victim of our own simple lust.

For whoever we are, no matter how high,
We never will cease to plot and connive.

Rejoicing as adversaries suffer and die,
Hatred is our wings, slaughter our flight.

Victory? Well, what does it mean?
Glory! However much you can glean.

For it's shallow, hollow, not worth the strife,
The death of those innocent, robbery of life.

But most chilling, appalling, barbaric of all,
How it continues, how, forever, men fall.

And what of this talked of 'supernatural force'?
Did He influence history to take this sad course?

Did He wish for Man to descend to such shambles?
We've wondered from the path, we're smothered in brambles.

So when He comes to survey His creation,
Expecting Utopia, universal elation,

All He will find is a great bloated vulture,
devouring the remains of a once-promising culture.

Hannes Whittingham (13)
Sawston Village College, Sawston

Through The Eyes Of A Leaf

Here I am, a little leaf,
falling to the ground,
here I am, a little leaf,
twirling all around.

Up above me is my tree,
which from now I quickly flee.

The time has come, the time is right,
for when I must complete my flight,
from the tree onto the ground,
twirling, twirling all around.

Crash! What was that?

There is my tree upon the ground,
soon to be thrown upon the mound,
the trees have been taken off to be turned into paper,
these people don't think what might happen later . . .

More trees are cleared to make space for cattle herds,
these people aren't exactly nerds!

Didn't they hear me? Didn't I say?
I shouted my warning loud and clear,
bellowed it loudly for all to hear.
Stop it, I tell you, stop it I say.
Act now, or soon we'll all be gone . . .

Duncan MacGregor (11)
Sawston Village College, Sawston

Explodron

The monster has a body like a mountain.
Eyes like fire.
A nose like a boulder.
A mouth like the Grand Canyon.
Legs like pillars
And arms like spears.
The monster is as fierce as a volcano.
As clever as dolphins.
As loud as a foghorn.
As smelly as fish
And as frightening as the end of the world.

The monster . . . Explodron.

Jake Hardwick (12)
Sawston Village College, Sawston

Next Generation

Trying to keep up
With all these new gadgets and stuff
Mobile phones and iPods
TVs and game consoles
DVDs, CDs and the rest
People buying only the best
I buy something new
And everyone comes to see what I've found
The next day a new model comes round
I'm back behind
I just can't keep up
With all these new gadgets and other stuff.

George Chapman (12)
Sawston Village College, Sawston

Generation

G oing out
E nergy high
N ever bored
E ating pie
R elaxing happily
A ll day long
T houghtless mind
I 'm never wrong
O nce again, it has gone
N ever to return, still feeling strong.

Amy Ornstien (13)
Sawston Village College, Sawston

Teenagers

PlayStation 3, mobile phones,
Computers and games,
Teenage hormones!

Boy bands, girl groups, chick flick movies
Newest iPod,
With songs so groovy!

Tiny tummies, trendy clothes,
Popular people -
What they say goes!

Gucci belts and Jane Nor' bags,
Top Shop trousers.
Glamorous people in glamorous mags.

Hair gel, facials, an ugly spot,
Shampoo and condition
That's the lot!

Teenage life, teenage stuff,
Teenagers' parents
Have had enough!

Cassie Cope (12)
Sawston Village College, Sawston

13th Birthday

My thirteenth birthday was recently
It could not have been much better,
I received many gifts and presents,
Not mentioning the letters.

All of my friends were round that day,
So they could celebrate with me,
We played outside on the Diablo,
But it was sadly too dark to see.

Man United were playing too
On the television,
It was a great feeling when we won,
It was no consolation.

The whole day was great
Plus Man U's victory,
I just hope they will win again,
Until they reach their glory.

Alex Batten (13)
Sawston Village College, Sawston

Rules, I Dream Of . . .

The rules I dream are the rules I hope for.
I dream that our generation will make a pledge,
to share our love with those in need of care.

In all the countries and the places the rules
should be that everyone has happy faces.

Remembering the rules we make
will make the world a happier place.

Emily Morris (11)
Sawston Village College, Sawston

Bullying

Have you ever felt so downhearted
because someone is upsetting you?

Have you ever been left out
or wanting to cry with tears?

Have you ever been threatened,
pushed around or even been verbally abused?

Do you have any friends at all?

Would you watch someone else
being tormented or crossing a busy road
to come to their aid?

This person could be you!

What would you do?

Philipp Scholtes (11)
Sawston Village College, Sawston

PE

In the subject PE
Children are as fast as fleas.
You run and you throw balls that weigh a tonne.
There are weird balls,
When you kick they will fall.
You jump in the deep end
And you can take turns with a friend.
You jump bars and posts
And then you boast.
No need to do this,
You've just got to miss.

Connor Ellis (12)
Sawston Village College, Sawston

Talkin' 'Bout My Generation

If I had a magic wand . . .
I would change the world so there was no poverty,
no homeless people,
no one dying of an illness,
no unloved animals.

If I had a magic wand . . .
I would change the world so there was no school uniforms,
no classrooms,
no homework,
only boys went to school.

If I had a magic wand . . .
I would change the world so there was no sadness,
no crying,
no anger,
no hating, no killing, fighting,
no *wars!*

Katie Lloyd (11)
Sawston Village College, Sawston

Mrs Anderson

Mrs Anderson is a great teacher
She is a bundle of fun, and is an extraordinary feature.
3 days a week she teaches us
With not at all a bit of fuss.

Mrs Anderson is very smart
And when she gets home she has a jam tart.
She is so funny, she makes us all laugh
And after her hard work, she has a warm bath.

Mrs Anderson is always bright
And when it's her birthday she's like a light.
Her hair is golden brown
And only Mrs Anderson deserves a jewelled crown.

Jordan Smart (11)
Sawston Village College, Sawston

The Phones

We sit staring
not moving a wink,
eyes fixed to the screen
not daring to blink.

The box-like thing is new to us,
makes a noise and a sound,
when we press a button
it makes our heart pound.

But when we press the button of doom
the screen fades away,
the sound goes silent
and yet again it is put away for another day.

Anna Tindall (12)
Sawston Village College, Sawston

Why?

You have hurt us.
You have left us to suffer,
Suffer the consequences of your injustice.
Why?

You have caught us in the sinister nets that frighten us,
Poured oil into our once clear seas,
Destroying our world so we have nothing left.
Why?

Do you find it fun to hurt us?
Do you enjoy destroying our homes?
This is your chance to change.
Why?

Ellis Stratton (11)
Sawston Village College, Sawston

Football Crazy

The players danced around each blade of grass.
The awesome player made a cracking pass.
The ball flew through the air like a thunderbolt.
The referee ran and drew to a halt.
He thrusts the red card in the face of the player.
Who screeched at the top of his voice, 'That's not fair!'

Jack Hayden (12)
Sawston Village College, Sawston

Modern Childhood

IPods and mp3s,
Not vinyls and cassettes,
Everything's digital,
No need to wind up!

E-mails and MSN,
No need for a stamp,
Mobile phones,
Slimline and compact.

It's all USA and Europe,
Forget Brighton and Yarmouth.
Fast planes and trains,
No diesels and steams.

PlayStations and Wiis,
Forget board and card games.
It's all on a computer,
No Trivial Pursuit.

Children are safeguarded,
Not free to roam wild.
Gone is the innocence
Of being a child.

Megan Salmon (12)
Sawston Village College, Sawston

In My Future

In my future are hover vehicles that fly between cities
Concealed by huge glass domes.
Buildings and towers made from gold,
Towering above, winking under two golden suns.

In my future the world is at peace,
With nations living together, side by side.

In my future animals are equal to humans
And cigarettes are banned.

In my future we've made contact with aliens,
So different species stop off at Earth,
But only in my future.

For now I have to deal with reality:
Boring buildings, wars, humans greater than animals,
But not for long,
Because in the future that's going to change.

Evelyn Roddom (11)
Sawston Village College, Sawston

Teenagers

All we get is disrespected.
For hanging around,
The police take our names down.
What is wrong with meeting a mate?

We're getting spots and becoming stressy.
We don't care if our room is messy.
Do we deserve all this upset?

We get told to think about our future.
We don't care about next year.
We've had enough.
What is wrong with enjoying *now*?

Fiona Case (12)
Sawston Village College, Sawston

Typical Teenager

I'm late for school,
I'm feeling stressed,
I can't find my homework
'Cause my room's a mess.

My skin is all greasy,
I'm drowning in spots,
I wanna have a shower
But still got to do lots.

I'm finally ready,
It's half-past 10,
I zoom straight out of the door
And run like a mad man.

I'm at the school,
I've got detention now,
I feel really sweaty
Like a black and white cow.

This is my life,
And it's always like this,
Maybe one day
I'll give school a miss.

Vivien Gu (11)
Sawston Village College, Sawston

Brain Rot TV

Sits in the corner rotting children's brains.
Staring at me irresistibly.
With all of its power pulling me in.
TV controller turning on the rays.
Am I controlling the television,
Or is it controlling me?

Emma Mounsey (11)
Sawston Village College, Sawston

The Things I Would Change

If I were the one, the one who ruled . . .
I would change the way some people disrespected others.
I would change the way people thought,
                        change how people believed.
I would change the way the world looked.
Change the expressions on the faces of buildings.
The colossal, unpleasant skyscrapers would become small
                        peaceful, happy cottages.

They wouldn't be destructive.
They would be thoughtful.
What I would most definitely change is the way
people destroyed the world I would create a whole new world.
A place where people looked before they leapt.
But the thing I would not change is the way people thought freely
                        and moved freely.

Tom Lucas (12)
Sawston Village College, Sawston

What Would You Do?

If I had a wand, a magical wand
I would change the world
By having no school
And eating all day
I would ask to be rich
And have loads of sweets
No homework to do
To stop the wars
And travel the world
Have a massive trampoline
Well that's what I would change.
What would you change?

Eleanor Fish (11)
Sawston Village College, Sawston

Who Am I?

Top-class jumper
Fantastic climber
Banana eater
Baby holder
Lightning runner
Fur coat wearer
Loud screamer
Who am I?

Áine Jones (12)
Sawston Village College, Sawston

My Cat Alfie

My cat likes his food
My cat likes his sleep
And he will be really scared
At the slightest peep.

To find the best seat in the house
You'll have to move the cat
It isn't as easy as it looks
He really is quite fat.

He sleeps on beds and under bushes
Not on anything higher
And in winter, he really likes
To sit beside the fire.

He's scared by noises, loud or quiet
Anything makes him jump
But he's also scared by kittens
And any type of bump.

He may be lazy, he may be fat
He may not move a single limb
But he's still my cat, the best cat
The best cat in the world, and I love him.

William Ingram (12)
Sawston Village College, Sawston

All Pink . . .

The strong, alcoholic nail varnish, perfect pink.
The tranquillity of her room, velvet curtains, all pink.
The fragrant roses in her garden, a gentle pink.
The blusher on her dressing table, tinted pink.
The lipstick in her handbag, glistening pink.
The scarf she wore on Sundays, a special pink.
The colour of her gentle tongue, pink.
The pen she used to write to her love, romantic pink.
The strawberries that she gave to me, pink.
All pink.

Georgie Bifulco (12)
Sawston Village College, Sawston

Fell The Wings Of Black

Black is the angel of death
As he screams out and cries,
Because the angels from Heaven
Have caused his demise.
His cushioned, fluffy throne
Is shredded to pieces
As God's black angel
Takes hold and seizes.
The freedom is gone
From this lonely king
As the angels from above
Flutter their wings.
His claws like devils' tridents
Scratch and screech,
Until the very last word
He will speak.
He's sentenced to death.
The poor angel cries,
For there's no escape
From his criminal lies.

Rebecca Bartram (12)
Sawston Village College, Sawston

Black Night

The night was black
With no bright moon,
The air was cold and clear,
And though it was the summer,
All was not warm and well,
For in the valley witches gathered
Around a fire of coal
To cast a curse this midsummer's night
Upon the young and old;
Against the glare on harpy,
With black silken thread for hair,
Threw back her head and said,
'Let's kill them all, the world will be ours
Evermore, for evermore.'
Shouts of cold delight and hard eyes gleaming,
But through the coals came a witch's cat,
Silent plea on his black furry face:
You cannot claim the world,
No plants, no life, no sea,
Just black, endless black, evil, death and pewter.
So they did scream at him, a simple cat,
Saviour of the Earth,
But the witches soon ceased to be angry.
Their screams turned to sobs,
The sun was rising, dazzling white
An angel in the east
To stop the black.
The black has ended.

Olivia Tigg (12)
Sawston Village College, Sawston

I Laugh, I Weep

I look upon this world
That I created with love and care,
I gave it its first breaths,
I gave it the tools for perfection,
I gave it food and drink,
And then they came,
My smiles warmed them,
To start with there was harmony,
Peace, silence,
But then they argued,
They made objects to hurt and kill,
To silence,
They started again, again and again,
Each time the missiles grew more extravagant,
Fire and flames dominated my sight,
I screamed, I wept,
First I asked, then I pleaded, I begged,
But they persisted,
Now they kill all,
The ones harbouring guilt
And the ones pure of heart,
They have not long
Before their time expires,
And no longer do they argue,
I looked upon this world
That I created with love and care.

Deborah Kendall (13)
Sawston Village College, Sawston

Need We Change The World?

The world was one of God's amazing creations,
Need we destroy it by bloody battles, fiery battles,
Cruelty to animals, destroying trees,
And most importantly ourselves?

The world was one of God's amazing creations,
Need we destroy it by building power plants to power our
electric goods,
Or even worse, cutting down our forests and destroying the animals
Just for paper to put on our desks?

The world was one of God's amazing creations,
Need we destroy it by starting unnecessary wars,
Feuds over resources like oil or coal?
But don't we know best?
Put it all behind and make this world a better place.

Sebastian Whittaker (11)
Sawston Village College, Sawston

Ocean

As the blue in the ocean shimmers
In the depth and coldness
I can see in the ocean's eyes,
I can see the loneliness,
I can see the sadness,
I can hear the ocean cry.
As I hear the ocean scream
I feel cold as ice cream.
As it clashes on the floor
It sounds like it is knocking on my door.

Austin Hill (12)
Sawston Village College, Sawston

The Children Of The Electronic Age

We are the children of the electronic age,
We rarely use the written page,
We talk to each other through the computer,
We love it cos it's much, much quicker!

We are the children of the electronic age,
The old record shops are in a rage.
Mums and dads look at us odd
Cos we download music to our iPod!

We are the children of the electronic age,
In outdoor sports we do not engage,
The thing that brings us hours of joy
Is playing games on our Game Boy!

We are the children of the electronic age,
As we grow up you war to wage,
Not against men at arms,
But climate change is doing harm!

Megan Pyle (11)
Sawston Village College, Sawston

Pink!

Pink is my valentine
That represents love,
This is the colour that makes me blush,
Pink is the colour for flushed,
When someone knows
That they are loved,
Pink is the colour
That lifts you above.
When you're sure that love is yours,
Pink is the colour you can adore,
For pink shall lift you up
From the floor!
Pink!

Holly Sondhi (12)
Sawston Village College, Sawston

Red

A beautiful rose
A punched nose
A warning sign
A *don't cross that line*
An angry face
A funky shoelace
A big desert mountain rock
A stripy sock
A broken heart
A tie to be smart
A strawberry fruit
A dangerous root
A cave painting design
A colour of wine
A cut that bled
Yep, you guessed it, red!

Mairi Bright (13)
Sawston Village College, Sawston

Blue

Blue like my bedroom
Bad like my cat
Bold like a felt-tip pen
Loud like my radio
Light like a feather
Undecided like a hard maths question
Undead like zombies
Exciting like me
Empty like my cupboard
Extraordinary like me again.

Ashley Cann (12)
Sawston Village College, Sawston

Rainbow

Red is the buses, the postbox, the anger
Orange is the carrots, the apricots, the mangoes
Yellow is the daffodils, the sun, the bees
Green is the envy, the jealousy, the bushes
Blue is the peace, the calm, the tranquillity
Indigo is the frustration, the butterflies, the ocean
Violet is the flowers, the plums, the summer evenings
Rainbows are beautiful, pretty and elegant.

R uby red
A mazing amethyst
I nteresting indigo
N eat navy
B eautiful blue
O ptimistic orange
W onderful white.

Claire James (12)
Sawston Village College, Sawston

Nightmares

The church bell chimes twelve
And you're all asleep!
Tucked up cosily in your bed
While nightmares go through your head!
Suddenly you hear footsteps on the stairs,
Then you hear them in your room!
You don't dare move an inch,
But you really need to, to get back
Your pillow that has fallen on the floor!
You turn on your light and find out it's your cat!
You turn your light off, close your eyes
And hope to have sweet dreams . . .
But will you?

Rebecca Saunders (12)
Sawston Village College, Sawston

SVC (LDN)

Walking to school with my mates this morning,
'Cause I'm getting ready for a new day,
I just can't help still yawning,
But I'll try to make it to my lessons OK.

Everything seems to go as it should,
But I have to make it to the top floor,
I wish it could be easier, oh I wish it would,
About an hour later I make it through the door.

You might gossip, you might muck around,
Walking round SVC playground.

'Sun is in the sky, oh why, oh why
Would I want to be anywhere else?
Sun is in the sky, oh why, oh why
Would I want to be anywhere else?'

When you look with your eyes,
Everything seems nice,
But you might get a big surprise
When you see it's twice as nice.

Now I'm giggling with all my friends,
Messing around with all our food,
Talking about all the latest trends,
I'm in a much better mood.

Now I'm working out all these sums,
But I really don't understand it,
I'd rather be back with my chums,
But I find that I just can't quit.

Keely Scapens (11)
Sawston Village College, Sawston

Black

A black cat stalks
A blackbird squawks
A blackness covers the sky.

A blackened breeze
Rustles blackened trees
A black owl flies on high.

A black dog barks
A black star sparks
A black rat scuttles by.

A depressed goth
Squashes a blackened moth
A black and blue child starts to cry.

A black owl hoots
A black star shoots
A blackness covers the sky.

A black cat slinks
A black boat sinks
A black star goes flying by.

Katherine Jeffery (12)
Sawston Village College, Sawston

Gold

The rays of sun on a summer's day,
The petals on the flowers in May,
The jewels that lie beneath the earth,
The flames reflected on the hearth,
The ring upon a woman's hand,
The colour of a beach's sand,
The princess's flowing hair,
The oil lamp's yellow-tinted glare,
The sunset mirrored on the sea,
The autumn leaves that fall on me.

Jessica Kelley (12)
Sawston Village College, Sawston

How Would You Change The World?

How would you change the world?
Stop war?
End famine?
What would you do?

How would you change the world?
No homework?
No school?
What would you do?

How far would you change the world?
Faster cars?
More roads?
What would you do?

How would you change the world?
Different people?
Socialism?
What would you do?

The world will always be the same:
Gentle seasides,
Pink sunsets,
The world will always be the same . . .

Unless . . .

Ben Gallienne (12)
Sawston Village College, Sawston

Pensioner Vs Barry Boy

An old woman rocks on her rocking chair,
Her woolly fleece, slippers and scented bear.
She knits on her chair and moans about yobs,
When Den dies on EastEnders she sobs and sobs.
She snuggles up in her soft old bed,
She looks at her clock. 'I'm late!' she said.

A barry boy drives his 'done up' car
At 50mph he speeds past the bar.
He rolls down the street acting all tough,
He shouts out the window, 'I'm buff and I'm rough!'
He plays loud music in the streets
And gets a lot of stick from OAPs!

The barry boy pulls up in his granny's drive,
He shouts through the letter box, 'Nan! You still alive?'
He goes in the house to see if she's all right,
When he wakes her up she gets a big fright.
He gives her a kiss and says, 'Goodnight,'
Then he walks out the door and turns out the light.

Callum Dunsmore (13)
Sawston Village College, Sawston

Summer Green

Green hills and dales,
Emerald vales,
Dancing in the wind.
Green eyes so bright,
A dragon in flight,
Stretching across the sky.
Green spiky holly,
The dress of a dolly,
Swaying in the breeze.

Phoebe Gilderdale (12)
Sawston Village College, Sawston

The Wind

Charging with powers beyond imagination
A torn grey cloak trails behind him,
His face grey and battered
But circles of red, his eyes,
Never seen but always felt,
In his wake trees rustle in fear
And animals scurry to safety,
His howl spreads a terrible fear
Into even the strongest of hearts,
He has an invisible axe
Felling trees and causing chaos,
Destroying homes for the sake of sin,
His only fear, stillness,
He is forever on the move,
Chasing peace away.

Simon Rolph (13)
Sawston Village College, Sawston

Darkness

Darkness is coming,
Creeping through your windows,

Shrouding everything in a cloak of gloom;
He scares the little babies in their cots.

Darkness, night's companion;
Joking together in the pitch-black,

Seeing how many children they can scare;
Their eyes black with evil,

Rejoicing in cries of fear,
Waiting for the dreaded sun to set,

The dreaded sun to set.

Jasmine Batters (13)
Sawston Village College, Sawston

The New Age

Mobile ringing
A car starting
Music blaring

Sounds of the new age
The touch of a button
And the world is in your hands

Washing machines
Computers
iPods

Do we need all this?

Global warming
Terrorism
Poverty

Do we need all this?

Jack Perry (11)
Sawston Village College, Sawston

Red

Red is the colour of anger and hate,
Red is the colour of murder and fate,
Red is the colour of death and pain,
Red is the colour of an old steam train,
Red is the colour of flames and fire,
Red is the colour of doom and dire,
Red is the colour of darkness and mystery,
Red is the colour of old war history,
Red is the colour of anger and hate,
Red is the colour of murder and fate.

Freddy Bennett (12)
Sawston Village College, Sawston

Colin Montgomerie

He whacks the ball from the tee,
See it fly into the tree.

Now it's landed in the rough,
This is going to be tough.

This has made Monty cross,
Usually he's the boss.

He makes a good fairway drive
On this long par five.

Oh no! It's rolled into the sand,
Not a very good place to land.

He chips it out with his wedge,
But it goes into a hedge.

Now he hits it on the green,
This looks a better scene.

His first putt skims just past the pin,
A second tap sends it in.

Then he picks up his club,
And he goes to the pub.

Charlie Wolfe (11)
Sawston Village College, Sawston

Alone At Night

This piece of fabric, his coat, his pillow and his bed
Sheltering him from deathly winds, protecting his china head.

His hands as cold as a freezer, his endlessly quivering jaw,
He huddles up for another night's sleep, another night on the floor.

His hair strewn and scrambled like spaghetti Bolognese,
All twisted up and terribly tangled in a never-ending maze.

His only light, the moon, shines down with a beam of hope,
As he sits alone, a little boy, trying very hard to cope.

Jessica Parish (12)
Sawston Village College, Sawston

My Generation

My generation can swing and sway,
'Cause we're the yesterday, tomorrow and today

MSN, Internet, mobiles and more,
All this high-tec law.

My generation can swing and sway,
'Cause we're the yesterday, tomorrow and today

Music is the theme of today,
That shows people the way.

My generation can swing and sway,
'Cause we're the yesterday, tomorrow and today

Sports, fashion, telly abounds,
And it is all around.

My generation can swing and sway,
'Cause we're the yesterday, tomorrow and today.

Merrill Hopper (11)
Sawston Village College, Sawston

Riddle

I am worn on people's feet
I really smell quite sweet
I'm made of many different colours
With a tick on my side
Billions of people wear me
There are many different types of me
Some running
Some boots
Some fashionable
but whatever you wear, you look cool!

Max Annetts (12)
Sawston Village College, Sawston

Unknowing

Sparks spraying,
burning,
fighting like a warrior,
penetrating heat,
solitary fire.

Pure mist
resonantly staying,
reverberating,
never forgiving,
never forgetting.

Eternal opposite,
the beginning,
the end,
forever and ever,
until he winds down

And stops the silence,
conscientious,
continuous,
truthful,
misleading.

Strong muscles,
brave heart,
fearless,
but with fear within,
cold numbness.

This is death
or maybe time.
It might be both.

Emily Cowling (14)
Sawston Village College, Sawston

A Lone Tear Dries

A lone tear dries.
I think of the creation,
When I used my hands to craft the valleys,
When I planted every tree,
When I filled the seas with my tears,
But now the lone tears dry.

I'm proud,
But disgusted,
So the tears begin to flow.

A lone tear dries.
I look down at my children,
Each unique, each designed by my will.
The next generation,
The one I designed differently,
The one that makes my lone tears dry.

I'm proud,
But disgusted,
So my tears begin to flow.

I let the lone tears slide.
The crash, the crash, the crash
Of the next generation's war.
The end of the world is coming,
As sure as a lone tear dries.

Diana Paulding (13)
Sawston Village College, Sawston

Things That Make Me Tick

Things that make me tick
Are the things that go so quick

Holidays by the sea
And learning how to ski

Parties with my friends
Where music is the trend

Playing football matches
Amazing rugby catches

Food I love to eat
Especially for a treat

Checking out the web
iTunes, YouTube, MSN

Diablo's the latest rage
Maybe it's just my age.

Simon Woodley (12)
Sawston Village College, Sawston

Me And My Friends

Me and my friends went to the cinema
Me and my friends made lots of litter
Me and my friends went to the park
Me and my friends made a dog bark
Me and my friends watched the clouds
Me and my friends read out loud
Me and my friends had a look
To see that we made havoc!

Michael Barker (12)
Sawston Village College, Sawston

The Nightmare Before Landing

Breathless as the sky fills with screams,
I shiver as I think of death,
Stuck in my grave for evermore,
As I sit inside this doomed plane.

It dips and turns in every way,
Only miracles stop its sway.
I finally let go of hope,
Although annoyed, I feel peaceful.
I know this struggle is my last
As we begin the death spiral.

I start to feel dizzy.
As the plane struggles to go on,
It starts to fall rapidly,
But nobody can stop this plane.

The next moment I sit, confused.
My dad wakes me as we land.
I'm not sure what happened up there,
I know for sure I have survived,
As my senses return slowly.

Robert Riley (13)
Sawston Village College, Sawston

My Riddle

I can be human or animal,
I'm made of stone or marble,
It's quite hard to miss me,
I'm in lots of places.
I can be big or I can be small.
What am I?

A: Statue

Nathan Hardwick (11)
Sawston Village College, Sawston

The Seasons

Imagine a house on a frosty morning,
Imagine a girl sweeping down the snow-carpeted pathway,
Hear the freshly iced grass of the village green crunching under
                                                    her feet,
Feel the harsh winter breeze hit her cheeks like daggers,
See the light patterned snowflakes rest gently on her eyelids,
Watch her lie in the grass by the icy lake as winter melts away . . .

Imagine a park on a breezy afternoon,
Imagine the crispy leaves crashing to the floor in slow motion,
Their ochre shimmer merging with the dusty rays of sun,
Hear them crash and crumble beneath the rubbery soles of her shoes,
Watch her dance and spin as she becomes the centre of a
                                                    leafy tornado,
See her waltz through the days until all the leaves have gone . . .

Imagine a field of golden buttercups in a gentle sunrise,
Imagine a burning red sun pushing its way past the hills,
Watch her gaze at the blossoming flowers of the new dawn,
Listen to the soft sound of the newborn lamb,
See the rays of light float in ambience around her,
Feel her eyes fall softly upon the glowing countryside . . .

Imagine a sandy beach at daybreak,
Imagine feeling the sun hit you and then disappear mysteriously,
                                        as if stolen by clouds,
Feel the grains of sand squeezing through her toes like rice,
Hear the soft rush of the tide rolling toward her,
See the distant ships steam across the straight horizon,
Watch her wrap up warm and wish as the sunshine hides away,
                                                    autumn is coming.

Autumn, winter, summer, spring,
You'll never know what the seasons might bring . . .

Emmeline Carr (12)
Sawston Village College, Sawston

If I Were Prime Minister For A Day . . .

If I were Prime Minister for a day,
there'd be many changes I would make.

If I were Prime Minister for a day,
there'd be a party with everyone invited.

If I were Prime Minister for a day,
everyone would have a good meal.

If I were Prime Minister for a day,
I'd fly to Florida and swim with the dolphins.

If I were Prime Minister for a day.
I'd fly up in a helicopter and throw money.

If I were Prime Minister for a day,
I'd build a big castle for all the homeless.

If I were Prime Minister for a day,
the ground would be one big trampoline.

If I were Prime Minister for a day,
sadness would be banned.

If I were Prime Minister for a day,
everyone would dance and sing and play
and scream and shout, 'Hip hip hooray!'

So why haven't I got any votes?

Nathalie Botcherby (13)
Sawston Village College, Sawston

My Family

M um, Dad, my brother and me
Y ears of generations have passed

F or my family to be here at last
A lthough a world of terror and violence we live
M y ancestors gave their lives to give us a gift so precious
I nspiration and admiration is what we should feel
L earn to love each other and
Y earn for some peace at last.

Chloe Griggs (11)
Sawston Village College, Sawston

Global Warming

The people don't care, they litter the streets,
They drive their cars and leave on the lights.

The animals care, their homes being destroyed,
While people are littering the Earth.

The factories don't care; they are on day and night,
Polluting the world with black sooty fumes.

The Poles certainly care, melting away,
Falling each day into the sea.

The cliffs certainly care, being eroded,
The sea wipes them away, gone forever.

The sky wants to help by changing the weather,
But no one is listening, so no one can care.

The people should care; they're killing their planet,
But still they don't notice, it just passes them by.

The ice caps are melting; the polars are dying,
The weather is changing; the cliffs are eroding,

But no one cares, they just let it happen.

Nicola Taylor (13)
Sawston Village College, Sawston

If I Could Change The World

I would stop the deadly wars and freeze global warming,
I would help the sick and poor and give the gold away,
I would shine the sun on the world and make everyone happy,
I would give the rain to those who need to drink, to live,
I would jump on hurricanes and soak up all the floods,
I would drive poverty away and dump it in the bin,
I would reload the melting ice caps and save the hungry polar bears,
I would win the lottery and give the money to Children in Need,
I would throw drugs away and burn every cigarette,
I would trap terrorism and heal and help the hurt.

Georgina Wright (11)
Sawston Village College, Sawston

Is This Our Generation?

Alcohol, drugs, violent crime,
Out on the streets; passing the time.
Fags, fights, chuck me some booze,
Are we really how they portray us on the evening news?

Shouting, abusing, stealing form a shop,
Singing too loudly to rap and hip hop.
Chucked out the cinema, thrown off the bus,
Is this how other generations perceive us?

Chilling out, chatting, listening to tunes,
Up in the pits of our messy rooms.
Laughing, joking, having fun,
Yeah, we're not perfect,
But we're only young.

Talking, eating, dancing away,
We're only teenagers who want to enjoy our day.
So give us a break, we won't pinch your beers,
We just want to have fun in our adolescent years!

Jessica Parish (13)
Sawston Village College, Sawston

Death

His heart of ice freezes the innocent in the darkness of the night,
His blank, gaunt face shows no emotion.
Life means nothing to him,
Just a light to be turned off.
His cloak of ash surrounds him,
He glides through the night searching for his next victims.
He laughs at the sorrow of others.
His pale skin stretched tightly across rotting bones,
He never smiles, never cries, feels no pain.
Passing through every life, making sure no one escapes his breath.

Ailise Smith (12)
Sawston Village College, Sawston

Generations

Working down the corner shop
Or selling junk on Ebay?
Reading 'The Famous Five'
Or watching 'The Simpsons' (Hooray!)?
Listening to Motown classics
Or head-banging to Metallica?
Getting caned six times
Or, 'Just apologise.'
'Sorry, Sir.'
Talking to your friend down the road (Bob!)
Or txtin ur m8 on ur nu mob?
Then . . .
Or now?
Which do you prefer?

Aidan Shields (12)
Sawston Village College, Sawston

Talkin' 'Bout My Generation

They used to have TVs, now we have PSPs,
They used to have post, now we have email,
They used to play marbles, now we play computer games,
They used to wash dishes, now we have dish washers,
They used to say, 'Sticks and stones may break my bones,
But words will never hurt me!'
Now we say, 'PS3s and phones may break my bones,
But texts will never hurt me!'
They used to play sport, now we still do,
They used to climb trees, now we still do,
They used to cook good food, now we still do.
We find out a lot when we're talkin' 'bout my generation!

Olly Wyse (11)
Sawston Village College, Sawston

Roses Are Dead

(Written in memory of my baby brother, Billy. XX)

The roses are dead,
The violets are through,
Though you are gone,
My heart beats for you.
The sky has gone grey,
The lightning is white,
It's the end of the day
Yet your eyes are still bright.
My life is a blur,
I can't see a thing,
And all that I know
Is the joy that you bring.
Your life was unfair
And now it is gone,
And all I can hear
Is death's plaintive song.

Lydia Chantler-Hicks (13)
Sawston Village College, Sawston

My Generation

Guns blazing,
Bullets flying,
Blood spurting,
Bodies collapsing,
But that's OK,
Life's a game,
You can always reset . . . can't you?

Walking down the road,
Headphones in my ears,
Nodding my head,
Glanced at the road,
It was clear,
Started to cross,
Bang, I'm dead!
But that's OK,
Life's a game,
You can always reset . . . can't you?

Dancing at the club,
The bloke comes over,
He offers me a tablet,
He looks OK,
I take it,
I'm addicted to Ecstasy,
But that's OK,
Life's a game,
You can always reset . . . can't you?

Adam Sear (14)
Sawston Village College, Sawston

My Generation

Bones poking out of skin,
Humans who resemble hot air balloons,
People who flash their money everywhere and anywhere,
Yet people struggling for pennies,
My generation - a generation of difference.

From playing games in the garden
To spending every spare second glued to a screen,
From people in fake Burberry and baggy trackies,
To people with messy hair and skinny jeans,
My generation - a generation of change.

People locked in their homes,
Too scared to leave in case of never coming back,
With bombings and stabbings,
And people's lips stitched up,
My generation - a generation of terror.

People high on drink and drugs,
Little resources left for us,
With global warming and terrorism,
And loads of other stuff,
My generation - a generation of mess.

Well your generation will be obsessed about my generation,
Just as my generation has been about the generations before,
And then you can make up your own mind about my generation.

Sophie Harris (15)
Sawston Village College, Sawston

Solitary Madness

Rugged street corner,
Gun in my hand,
Murder of a child
And I don't give a damn.

Drugs drive me on,
When I'm lost or alone,
Depression, just a joke,
On the streets that I roam.

I demand respect,
For my hidden Visage,
The hoodie obscuring,
My tainted scars.

I need it, I want it,
You're in my way,
Now I'm gettin' crazy,
Don't provoke me today.

The blood of the kid,
Smeared on my hands,
I'm murderer now,
And I don't give a damn.

Zuhair Crossley (13)
Sawston Village College, Sawston

Daydream In The Train

I closed my eyes
And went into a land
Where poppies grew on the lake
And water lilies in the sand.
I opened my eyes and
There I was sitting in the train.
It's strange that when you close your eyes
You can travel with no aim.

Eleanor Eloya (11)
Sawston Village College, Sawston

Gut-Wrenching Green

As the snot drops
It's sickening
To a slimy slush pea soup
Overflowing the bowl
Forming an oozy green swamp
Oozing out of the green keyhole
Creeping down
Like a horror movie coming to life
As if it was a slushy radioactive swamp monster
Drowning its victims helplessly.

Carl Sadler (13)
Sawston Village College, Sawston

Unique

(Based on the book 'Unique' by Alison Allen-Gray)

They told me I was an only child. Unique,
They wanted me to be clever,
Mum and Dad wanted me to be like him . . .
My dead brother who had the name and looks,
They lied.
Mum and Dad lied, kept him a secret.
His best friend and tutor kept him a secret,
Kept me a secret . . .
How could they?
How could they lie?
But now, I wish I hadn't discovered the truth above him,
About me,
I'm not unique,
I'm a copy,
An experiment . . .
A clone.

Emma Bright (11)
Woodland Middle School, Flitwick

Unique

(Based on the book 'Unique' by Alison Allen-Grey)

Once I thought life was just difficult
That I would have to face it
But now I know the truth
And now I have to run
Hide away from me
Hide away for Mum
Dad's tracking me
But it's all his fault
I'm unique
Just because I'm not.

I can't be anywhere
And *they* can find me here
I feel as if I'm drowning
I know that I'm a lie
All I am is a body
Just a 'duff' repeat
This is *his* bone with *his* flesh
I'm merely his rubbish clone
I'm unique
Even though I'm not.

So no one knows I'm here
I hope they never will
All I want is *my* life
But it's all too late
I'm not even *me* anymore
I'm unique
And the only one who's not.

Phoebe Wilsmore (11)
Woodland Middle School, Flitwick

Through The Eyes Of . . .

An old man,
The world would seem so great,
From technology to pizza,
Everything is so advanced.

All the man remembers is
His own childhood,
Even though it's fading,
He still remembers
The little black steam train,
That took him to the seaside.

Now he has no memory,
So he waits for the boy,
Who he seems to remember,
Something niggles in his mind
Who is this boy?
As the boy cuts the man's hair.

Slowly the man thinks
I know this boy
but then the thought slips,
And he is left, once again
An old man with years of
Long-forgotten memories,
And the boy,
Everything was so simple!

Frankie Finn (12)
Woodland Middle School, Flitwick

Clones

(Based on the book 'Unique' by Alison Allen-Gray)

Clones; the mirror image of a life form
Forever stealing the identity of the first
Hiding behind a curtain of truth
Their lives forever cursed.

Clones; always living in a shadow
Their way through life already chosen
Always in second place
As if one before has spoken.

Clones; trying to meet expectations
Failing where others did succeed
Looking for approval
A basic human need.

Luke Browne (12)
Woodland Middle School, Flitwick

Living Life To The Full

(Based on the book 'Unique' by Alison Allen-Gray)

Have you ever wondered why you're here and what your purpose is
Or why we carry on with our petty little lives?
The answer isn't to do with money or making massive gains.
It's to live your life to the full.

Your purpose here is to be unique, to be your own good person.
To enjoy your life and to have a grin on your face until the day you die.
To live your life to the full.

What happens when you die?
It's the question nobody can answer.
Is there never-ending calm or do you go to Heaven or Hell?
One thing that we can say for sure is that if you've lived your life
to the full
It really doesn't matter.

Thomas Harrison (11)
Woodland Middle School, Flitwick

The Only One
(Based on the book 'Unique' by Alison Allen-Gray)

I'm sitting here, in a dark corner, cold, alone and miserable.
Scared to step outside, terrified of people discovering what I am.
They would just point and laugh at me if they knew.
Call me names, freak, weird and abnormal.
I'm the only one.
I wish I never knew, I could have been happy right now.
Yet I'm stuck in a dark, cold, gloomy room.
I *hate* the person who has done this to me.
I wish I could just be normal.
But no they made me in a lab, I'm a duff copy of my brother.
I'm a *clone,* the only one.

Holly Barber (11)
Woodland Middle School, Flitwick

Unique, I Am Not
(Based on the book 'Unique' by Alison Allen-Gray)

Unique I am not, not a one-off,
I'm one of a pair
Quite a weird thing to be.
Unique I am, not
Everyone,

Isn't it weird to see?

A difference there is between
My peers and my family,

No one is just like them,
Obvious to the eye.
To them I am just me.

Ellena Gazeley (11)
Woodland Middle School, Flitwick

Looking Through My Eyes . . .
Or Yours?

(Based on the book 'Unique' by Alison Allen-Gray)

Living such a perfect life
Unknowing that it's full of lies
Seeing all the wonders
But secretly they are not mine
Seeking for the answers
Although they are already found.

The truth is out, everyone knows
They're good at hiding it but now it's all exposed.

There is only one reason for me to live,
To replace
No one cares how I feel,
It's just about them
Maybe just maybe I can have my own life
And one day be free
But this is just dreaming.

I'm just a duff copy of the original
Not unique
Not different

This is not me,
This is not my life

These are not my eyes I look through every day,
This is not my perfect life, it's someone's lies.

Victoria Abbott (11)
Woodland Middle School, Flitwick

Double Trouble

(Based on the book 'Unique' by Alison Allen-Gray)

I can't believe it, I had a brother and I didn't even know
And then when I asked my mum, she put on a show
The weird thing was he looked just like me
And everyone else seemed to agree

I wanted to investigate and find out
As much as I possibly could about
The brother I never knew I had
Because I couldn't ask my mum and dad

What university did he go to?
What subjects did he do?
A prize in science he did get
This brother of mine I wish I'd met.

I went to his university, Cambridge it was
To meet the teachers that taught him because
I wanted to find out and discover
As much as I could about my new found brother.

Mr Nicholls told me my brother was in Grenville Hall
Apart from that, not much else at all
Except for the fact one sad day
My new found brother had passed away.

Nick Welton (11)
Woodland Middle School, Flitwick

Dominic

I always thought I was just a normal boy . . .
Till the day I found out my parents were hiding something from me,
It all started with a photo,
Just a normal photo,
But then things just got more complicated,
People I loved were keeping secrets from me,
Secrets that could change my life forever.
I found out I had a brother,
A brother that was everything I wasn't,
Everything people wanted me to be,
They wanted me to be just like him,
Then I found out who I really was,
I was a freak,
I was just an experiment,
For all these years I knew nothing,
Now I'm not normal,
I'm different,
I'm a replacement for him,
I'm not myself anymore,
I'm just a copy of the best.

Katie Veryard (11)
Woodland Middle School, Flitwick

Through The Eyes Of Domonic

(Based on the book 'Unique' by Alison Allen-Gray)

I used to think that everyone was unique,
But now people taunt me, call me a freak.
Now no one believes me, I feel empty and alone,
My life spun around now I know I'm a clone.

Imagine your body, identical on each side,
A replica of your brother, after he died.
I was an experiment, born in a lab,
Even my birthmark's the same, a long swollen stab.

Living as a clone, there's pressure and stress
Just knowing me causes a monstrous mess.
An unnatural being, a lab rat, a 'thing'
The urge to tell my secret like a scorpion's sting.

My secret must be kept confidential, under lock and key,
People are still hunting, searching for me.

Charlotte Haimes (12)
Woodland Middle School, Flitwick

Young Writers Information

We hope you have enjoyed reading this book - and that you will continue to enjoy it in the coming years.

If you like reading and writing poetry drop us a line, or give us a call, and we'll send you a free information pack.

Alternatively if you would like to order further copies of this book or any of our other titles, then please give us a call or log onto our website at www.youngwriters.co.uk

Young Writers Information
Remus House
Coltsfoot Drive
Peterborough
PE2 9JX

(01733) 890066